THE GULF CRISIS

THE GULF CRISIS

An Attempt to Understand

Ghazi A. Algosaibi

KEGAN PAUL INTERNATIONAL
London and New York

First published in Arabic 1991 (1412 AH)
First published in English in 1993 by
Kegan Paul International Ltd
PO Box 256, London WC1B 3SW, England

Distributed by
John Wiley & Sons Ltd
Southern Cross Trading Estate
1 Oldlands Way, Bognor Regis
West Sussex PO22 9SA, England

Routledge, Chapman & Hall Inc.
29 West 35th Street
New York, NY 10001, USA

This translation © Ghazi A. Algosaibi 1993

Set in 10 on 12 pt Palatino by Intype, London
Printed in Great Britain by
TJ Press, Padstow, Cornwall

British Library Cataloguing in Publication Data
Algosaibi, Ghazi A.
Gulf Crisis: Attempt to Understand
I. Title
956.7044

ISBN 0–7103–0459–5

Library of Congress Cataloging-in-Publication Data
Quṣaybī, Ghāzī ʿAbd al-Raḥmān.
[Azmat al-Khalīj. English]
The Gulf Crisis: an attempt to understand / Ghazi A. Algosaibi.
p. cm.
ISBN 0–7103–0459–5
1. Persian Gulf War, 1991. 2. Persian Gulf Region—Politics and
government. 3. Hussein, Saddam, 1937– . I. Title.
DS79.72Q7513 1992
956.704'42—dc20
92–26232
CIP

I am indebted to Mr Peter Mansfield
for his invaluable help in the
translation of this book from
Arabic.

CONTENTS

Oh ye who believe! Stand up firmly for Allah, as witnesses to fair dealing, and let not the hatred of others make you swerve to wrong and depart from justice. Be just: that is next to piety: and fear Allah. For Allah is well acquainted with all that ye do.

The Noble Quran, Surah V, al-Maʾidah.

[This Quranic verse is taken from the translation of The Holy Quran by ʿAbdullah Yusuf ʿAli]

To H. I. K. and the other members of the 'battalion'.

1
THE DECISION

He who can take
Will not beg.

al-Mutanabbi [died 965]

Decision-making is an extremely complex process involving many factors. These include objective and subjective, permanent and temporary factors, matters of interest and principle, the facts of history and the laws of geography. All of these factors interact within the decision-maker's mind. The decision-maker's psychological make-up plays a decisive role in sifting through the various factors, discarding one and focusing on another, until a decision is finally reached – a decision which initially seemed as though it were spontaneous, easy and immediate.

Perhaps the most obvious indication of the complexity of the decision-making process is the hesitation which we sense in those around us and in ourselves before making any decision, regardless of how small it is. One decides to travel on a specific date, then cancels the trip, but then goes back to the original date. One decides to send a child to a certain school, then selects another school, then returns to the first choice, finally deciding on yet a third school. A woman hesitates before choosing a dress, or a piece of furniture or jewellery, for example, and this is a source of consternation for the salesperson. Any decision, regardless of its triviality, is the outcome of an interaction between many, sometimes contradictory, considerations.

The quest for any single reason to explain the decision by Iraqi President Saddam Hussein to invade Kuwait is at worst intentionally misleading and at best an oversimplification, regardless of whether it is suggested by a friend or an enemy of the Iraqi president. The 'insanity' of which Saddam Hussein's enemies speak does not explain what happened. Nor can a sincere desire to 'return the branch to the root' (i.e., return Kuwait to Iraq) sufficiently explain what happened. The truth of the matter is that many factors were behind the decision, including the personality of Saddam Hussein himself, conditions in Iraq following the war with Iran, factors related to the wider Arab arena, international politics, and the state of Iraqi–Kuwaiti relations. Without examining the interaction of these factors, it is impossible to obtain a full or clear picture of the background and dimensions of the decision.

Let us begin with what we consider to be the most important factor: Saddam Hussein's psychological make-up. Without this 'filter' through which the final decision had to pass, all the other factors cannot explain what happened in August 1990. Three characteristics of the Iraqi leader's psychological composition concern us in this regard. The first is his burning thirst for power and the greatness that is produced by power. The second is his constant inclination toward adventurism, and the third is the persecution complex imbedded in his psyche.

Since his earliest youth, Saddam Hussein has exhibited a clear tendency toward the pursuit and accumulation of power. Psychologists can determine the role played in this by his childhood, and sociologists can study the role played by his social environment. It suffices here to conclude that, since adolescence, he has been a leader. Initially, he was the leader of a gang of youths who intimidated the residents of his quarter. He then became a leader who imposed respect for himself on the other students in his school. He then became the leader of the group that was charged with assassinating 'Abd al-Karim Qasim (in history if not in reality). He then became the leader of a party. Finally, he became the sole leader of Iraq.

Adventurism is the means which he used to obtain power and greatness. We can say, in fairness to the facts, that every achievement accomplished by Saddam Hussein has been based on adventurism of one type or another. His acquisition of his first pistol when he was an adolescent was an adventure. Already a teenager, his entry into school was an adventure. His decision to join the Ba'ath Party was an adventure. His participation in the attempt to assassinate 'Abd al-Karim Qasim was an adventure. His escape from jail was an adventure. His return to Iraq to engage in party activity was an adventure. The first coup was an adventure. The coup overturning the coup was an adventure. The deposing of Ahmad Hasan al-Bakr was an adventure, and the war with Iran was an adventure.

In reviewing each important turning-point in Saddam Hussein's life, we find that a decision to embark on an adventure lies behind each one. None of these decisions was made by chance or haphazardly. Nor were they the result of the passive interaction of influential factors and changes. Rather, they were carefully calculated initiatives fraught with dangers. A political leader may be compelled from time to time to undertake an adventure. However, adventurism is the customary, natural style of Saddam Hussein's decisions. Accordingly, the decision to invade Kuwait is not unique. It is merely one link in a long, provocative chain of adventures.

Saddam Hussein's constant quest for greatness through continual engagement in adventures is incomprehensible if we neglect a third feature in his psyche, namely his profound feeling of being persecuted. Decisions which appear to others as a blind passion for greatness and a destructive love of adventure appear to Saddam Hussein as no more than a natural quest for security and peace. Saddam Hussein, in his own view, has always been and will always be in a state of legitimate defence, be it self-defence or defence of the regime, homeland or honour (these things are virtually bound together in his outlook). Others describe Saddam Hussein's behaviour as adventurism. He himself views his positions as having been taken in self-defence under duress.

Hence, his attempt to assassinate ʿAbd al-Karim Qasim was in defence of freedom against authority. His escape from prison was to defend himself against execution. The first coup was in defence of the homeland. The second coup was in defence of the Baʿath Party. The agreement with the Kurds and the violation of that agreement were both defensive measures to preserve Iraq's unity. The Algiers agreement with Iran in 1975 and the war in 1980 were legitimate acts to perpetuate the regime. One must neither sneer nor scoff at Saddam Hussein's repeated statements that he was compelled to invade Kuwait in order to defend Iraq, because he actually perceived matters in this way or something close to it.

We will now turn to the Iraqi–Iranian war, because it is the main background to the invasion of Kuwait. The complicated, historical problems between Arabs and Persians no doubt played a role in the conflict. However, it would do no justice to the truth to depict the war as an ethnic confrontation between the Arab and Persian nationalities. Sectarian considerations no doubt have some weight. But talk of a Shi'ite–Sunni war is unconvincing. Most of the Iraqi army are Shi'a. The border problem between Iraq and Iran came into the picture, but this does not make the war a mere violent border dispute. It would be more precise to say that all of these factors exploded when the Islamic revolution in Iran adopted the principle of exporting the revolution. This convinced the Iraqi president that being satisfied with the position of an observer would lead to his downfall and the liquidation of his regime. He resorted to his customary method, adventurism, by entering into a war with Iran, believing that an attack against Iran was really no more than active self-defence.

Gradually, with the ebb and flow of the war, the reasons and justifications for the war multiplied, not only in the Iraqi media, but, most importantly, in the mind of the Iraqi president. The war waged by Saddam Hussein in defence of his regime turned into a war to protect the 'eastern gateway to the Arab nation'. The wavering of any Arab's support anywhere became tantamount to national betrayal. The war into which Saddam Hussein entered based on narrow personal interests became a war to defend the Gulf in the face of an Iranian attempt to invade it. Iraq, in Saddam Hussein's view, was waging a war for the Gulf and on behalf of the Gulf. It was logical in such a situation for Iraq to expect the Gulf countries to consider the war their war and to contribute to it the same lives and money being contributed by Iraq. It mattered little to Saddam Hussein that the Arab nation did not endorse the war being waged in defence of its eastern gateway, or that no one in the Gulf asked him to attack Iran in order to defend the Gulf. Our current discussion concerns perceptions. If this was the impression that was etched in the Iraqi president's mind, referring to the facts is a waste of time, because, in the world of politics, as in the everyday world, the mental picture of reality, not reality itself, is what matters.

Saddam Hussein expected, in the light of the political chaos in Iran and the fragmentation of its army, that the war would end within weeks; the Iranian threat to his regime would be ended, and Iraq would be given full sovereignty over the Shatt al-Arab waterway. Actually, the Iraqi army was able at the start of the war to penetrate rapidly and occupy large areas of Iranian territory. However, the external danger posed by Iraq united domestic forces that were fighting with each other within Iran, and Teheran was able to stop the Iraqi penetration and shift to the offensive. After two years of war the Iraqi army had been sorely tried by major setbacks. This compelled Saddam Hussein to withdraw his forces into Iraq, and the offensive war turned into a true, not a figurative, defensive war. Had Iran been satisfied with its achievements at this point and agreed to peace negotiations, the course of events in the region would have been different. However, the Iranian leader, Ayatollah Khomeini, was determined to punish Saddam Hussein by toppling and liquidating his regime and establishing in Iraq an Islamic republic based on the Iranian model. This led to the continuation of the war for six more years, during which Saddam Hussein built up an enormous military force and gained considerable Arab and international sympathy. In 1988, Iraq's superior military technology was able to balance Iran's manpower superiority. Iraq repeatedly struck at Iran, compelling it to accept a cease-fire.

As soon as the Gulf countries, which were not enthusiastic about the war and feared its effects, found themselves in the same trench with Saddam Hussein, it became clear to them that the defeat of Iraq would mean Iranian hegemony over the Gulf, which would threaten all of the Gulf regimes. Thus, the Kingdom of Saudi Arabia provided Iraq with $26 billion, Kuwait provided $12 billion, Qatar and Abu Dhabi provided smaller sums, and various facilities were provided to Iraq (including road and port services and oil loans). Here, we are faced by one of the ironies with which the history of the crisis abounds: while the Gulf countries believed that they had given Iraq all that they could, the Iraqi president believed that these countries had given only a little.

In the wider Arab world, Yemen and Jordan supported Iraq, Syria and Algeria were aligned with Iran, and the other Arab countries were content to observe what was happening without enthusiasm for one side or the other. However, the Iraqi media succeeded day after day in presenting the Iraqi president as the 'Arab knight' standing alone to confront Persian anti-Arab expansion. As Iran escalated pressure on Iraq, sympathy for the Iraqi president grew. At the end of the war, Saddam Hussein emerged on the Arab scene as the most prominent Arab leader without a rival.

The position of the superpowers and the industrialized nations on the Iraqi–Iranian war can in general be summarized by the famous Arab proverb: 'Although I did not order it, it did not displease me.' Iran, with its revolutionary, extremist regime and determination to subvert wherever its influence extended, posed a threat to the interests of the United States and the Soviet Union alike. When the war began to incline in favour of Iran, and an Iraqi defeat seemed likely and imminent, the superpowers and the industrialized nations in general became clearly aligned with Iraq. This alignment took the form of the supply of advanced weapons, credit facilities, and sensitive military information that was poured into Iraq and denied to Iran. Here, we come to a second amazing irony: this huge arsenal which the East and West banded together to provide to Iraq is the same arsenal which the East and West are banding together to destroy.

The American position in sympathy with Iraq began to assume growing importance in the course of events. 'Irangate' occurred as an ingenious attempt to equip Iran with a limited quantity of American weapons in exchange for the release of the hostages being held by organizations loyal to Iran in Lebanon. This attempt was outside of general US policy. No sooner had it ended than it caused President Ronald Reagan and his aides endless difficulties. With the escalation of the tanker war, the American navy entered into a direct confrontation with Iran that ended with the destruction of a third of the Iranian navy and a number of oil platforms and the downing of a civilian passenger plane. This blatant military intervention against Iran was among the reasons that compelled Ayatollah Khomeini to accept a cease-fire. In the atmosphere of American–Iraqi rapprochement, it happened that an Iraqi military aircraft attacked an American frigate with a missile, killing a number of persons. None the less, the incident was allowed to pass quietly.

Iran announced that the war had ended with an Iranian victory, while Iraq declared that it was the victor. Each of the two sides was correct to some extent. If we remember that Iraq first attacked Iran and occupied Iranian territory, and that

Iran was able to repel the attack, we can speak of an Iranian victory. If we take into account that Iran, after it forced the Iraqi army to retreat into Iraq, assumed an offensive position and was able to occupy the Faw peninsula and threaten Basrah, and that Iraq was able to resist and then repel the attack, Iraq's talk of victory is understandable. As for the truth, as viewed by an objective, impartial observer, the war ended where it began, after material losses for Iraq close to $300 billion and Iran, according to its own estimate, $1,000 billion, with human losses on both sides estimated at a million persons, including casualties and prisoners.

While the Iraqi media were speaking of a great victory and the 'creator of victory' (i.e., Saddam Hussein), the Iraqi president was finding the taste of this victory extremely bitter. Saddam Hussein was unable to extend Iraq's sovereignty over the entire Shatt al-Arab waterway (the declared reason for the war). Nor was he able to change the Iranian regime threatening his regime (the true reason for the war). The Arab nation did not recognize Iraq's role in protecting its eastern gateway. Saddam Hussein emerged from the war as the most prominent Arab leader, but no one regarded him as the only Arab leader. The Gulf countries were not supporting him as he had hoped, i.e. with every conceivable sacrifice, military bases, and alliances. Iraq emerged from the war encumbered by $80 billion in debts and an army of more than a million men whom the exhausted Iraqi economy was unable to absorb in civilian jobs.

Amid this frustration and in the throes of these problems, in the darkness of the night Kuwait seemed to rise and glimmer like the legendary ring of Solomon, beckoning to Saddam Hussein, as if it were imploring him to take it – an act which would end all his crises at a single bold stroke, with a single courageous adventure. Saddam Hussein is a man who cannot resist such a temptation.

In Saddam Hussein's view, Arab circumstances were entirely suited to the idea. Egypt's isolation following its separate peace with Israel pointed to a clear imbalance in the Arab world that would permit the Iraqi president to play an Arab role that exceeded his capabilities and those of Iraq. Even when Egypt returned to the Arab fold, it did so under Iraqi patronage. Saddam Hussein thought this sufficient to ensure that Egyptian president Husni Mubarak would remain in his position as

11

a younger brother in the Arab family in which Saddam Hussein gave himself the position of the eldest brother. When the Arab Co-operation Council, which included Egypt, Iraq, Jordan and Yemen, was formed with the active co-operation of the Palestine Liberation Organization (PLO), Saddam Hussein felt certain that he had gained popular support in the eastern Arab countries for better or for worse. Regarding the countries of the Arab Maghreb (the North African Arab countries), Saddam Hussein was able, by various means ranging from direct gifts and literary prizes to intellectual seminars, effectively to penetrate various party, media, trade union and cultural organizations in a way that made him confident that public opinion in these countries would support him regardless of the positions of their governments. Throughout the Iraqi–Iranian war, Iraqi intelligence and party agencies were engaged in intensive efforts that went beyond the Arab world to the Islamic world. This activity entailed the recruitment of friends and the neutralization of enemies. The Iraqi president was able to take advantage of these 'investments' when zero hour for the invasion approached.

It seemed to Saddam Hussein that international opinion was hinting that it would bless the invasion of Kuwait. Saddam Hussein believed that guaranteeing the flow of oil at low prices would suffice, after a reasonable period of time, to convince the United States to accept the *fait accompli*. Nothing indicated that the American reaction would be a damaging military confrontation that might end in the death of thousands of American soldiers. Saddam Hussein's relationship with the Soviet Union was on the whole excellent. According to his calculations it was not likely that the Soviet Union would defend a state such as Kuwait, lying as it does within the American sphere of influence, against an old ally like Iraq, especially after the setbacks faced by the Soviet Union due to the collapse of communist regimes in Eastern Europe and the onset of economic difficulties in the Soviet Union itself. The Iraqi president thought that he would be providing the Soviet Union with a golden opportunity to prove to the entire world, particularly the United States, that it was still an effective superpower. With the neutralization of the United States and the Soviet Union in this way, it was unlikely that the other industrialized countries would undertake a military action against Iraq.

Kuwait seemed to be an exceedingly easy prey. Its armed

forces were incapable of mounting even symbolic temporary resistance. Kuwait was not bound to the United States by any security pact. Saddam Hussein did not forget that when Kuwait was compelled to request American protection of its tankers in the final phase of the Iraqi–Iranian war, it did not permit American warships to enter its territorial waters or American helicopters to land in its territory. Kuwaiti society was heaving with intense political activity as the result of the democratic revolutions in Eastern Europe and the emergence of political pluralism as the strong wave of the future. This activity was represented in the Kuwaiti opposition's mobilization of ordinary Kuwaitis to demand the return of the elected National Assembly which the amir disbanded four years before. Saddam Hussein concluded from the domestic political situation in Kuwait that he would receive a big welcome there, at least from the opposition. Also, there was a long-standing Iraqi claim to Kuwait, which reached a peak when ʿAbd al-Karim Qasim declared that Kuwait was an 'Iraqi district' and announced Iraq's resolve to reclaim it following Kuwait's independence in 1961. ʿAbd al-Karim Qasim was compelled to retreat under international and Arab pressure that took the form of the despatch of international and Arab forces to Kuwait. Successive subsequent Iraqi governments, including Saddam Hussein's own, have sought to leave vague the subject of final borders between the two countries, perhaps in expectation of an appropriate opportunity to renew the claims.

Several months after the Iraqi–Iranian war ended, Saddam Hussein dispatched Dr Saʿdun Hammadi to the Kingdom of Saudi Arabia and Kuwait to ask them for a 'loan' amounting to $10 billion to cope with post-war problems. The kingdom promised to examine the matter, whereas Kuwait offered to provide a modest sum representing a small percentage of the amount requested. Saddam Hussein immediately rejected the offered sum. He believed that it was offered to humiliate him deliberately. If we add to that Kuwait's refusal to cancel Iraq's debts,[1] the Kuwaiti Finance Ministry's reminder to the Iraqi

[1] From Kuwait's viewpoint, there was no Kuwaiti demand for the repayment of Iraq's debts owed to Kuwait. There was therefore no justification for Iraq's demand to cancel them. Moreover, Kuwait said that keeping Iraq's debts recorded officially would help Iraq convince other creditors to take account of circumstances.

Finance Ministry, in a routine manner, of accounts to be settled completed the picture of Kuwaiti provocation. When Kuwait refused to respond favourably to Iraq's request to decrease Kuwaiti oil production in order to enable Iraq to sell a larger amount of its oil, what appeared to the Iraqi president as a Kuwaiti provocation became a blatant act of aggression.

Those who spoke in retrospect of the 'stupidity, foolishness, and insanity' of the decision to invade were forgetting that the scenario revealed by events had not been the only or the most probable scenario. Saddam Hussein was well aware that he was embarking on a major adventure. However, international circumstances, as they appeared to him, did not indicate to him that he was moving towards certain suicide. What happened then? How did his calculations miss the mark? Why were his estimates incorrect?

We should remember two important facts about the Iraqi president. First, he is a first-rate 'tactical' manoeuvrer. However, his 'tactical' capability is not supported by a clear strategic vision, as has been proved time after time. Second, the Iraqi president, despite the media myth that has made him the 'author' of dozens of books, has limited education, and his knowledge of the world outside Iraq is inaccurate. He has almost no knowledge of Western democracies. Saddam Hussein did not discover that the elephant is the logo of the US Republican Party until November 1990. In a television interview with an American journalist, he expressed amazement when she informed him that critics of the American president are not punished. In another television interview he expressed his belief that the American president no longer has authority, because all his authority is 'distributed' to the chairmen of the boards of major capitalist companies!

Saddam Hussein was certain that there would be a 'strong' American reaction after the invasion. However, it did not occur to him that it would take the form of half a million American soldiers standing on his borders within several weeks. The Iraqi president was not able to analyse correctly the personality of American President George Bush. He thought him to be a 'second edition' of President James Carter, who was eager to avoid military confrontations, or of Ronald Reagan, whose military confrontations were limited to an air raid and the occupation of a city no larger than one of Baghdad's districts.

Saddam Hussein expected the United States to undertake 'Carter-like' measures that would not go beyond a boycott, or 'Reagan-like' measures that would not go beyond the dispatch of warships or possible reprisal air raids. He was completely prepared to confront such reactions. Shortly before the invasion, when Saddam Hussein met in Baghdad with the American ambassador, who was summoned to a meeting without warning and did not have specific instructions from her government, the American ambassador expressed the American government's desire to maintain good relations with Iraq, at which point Saddam Hussein became certain that the US reaction would remain on a scale which he could absorb.

The second mistake made by Saddam Hussein involves his misunderstanding of the personality of King Fahd Bin 'Abd al-'Aziz, despite his close relation with the Saudi king. Saddam Hussein had noticed that King Fahd, even at the peak of Iran's ascendancy during the Iraqi–Iranian war, had categorically refused to allow the United States to use bases and facilities on Saudi territory. Those closely familiar with the Saudi monarch know that he is peaceful and friendly by nature, and that he is willing to go to great lengths to save his country from the misfortunes of wars and crises. They also know that he defers painful, difficult decisions for as long as possible. Saddam Hussein exploited King Fahd's visit to Iraq after the end of the Iraqi–Iranian war. The visit was made at the urging of the Iraqi president, who arranged a warm official and popular reception for the king. He asked the king to sign a 'non-aggression' pact between the kingdom and Iraq. The request seemed extremely strange to the king, who thought that the relationship between the kingdom and Iraq, and between him and the Iraqi president, went beyond non-aggression to an alliance or a quasi-alliance. None the less, the king found it very difficult to refuse his host's request and consented to the pact. Saddam Hussein, armed with his knowledge of the genuine, peaceful intentions of the Saudi king and the new pact, was confident that the kingdom would not permit its territory to be transformed into a battlefield regardless of the circumstances.

The third mistake made by the Iraqi president was that he did not understand what was happening in the Soviet Union. President Mikhail Gorbachev had initiated an extensive reform programme on which depended not only his personal future, but that of the Soviet Union and the Communist Party as well. President Gorbachev was convinced that this programme could only succeed with effective co-operation from the West, which is led by the United States. This co-operation was not to be limited to ending the Cold War and its symptoms. It was also to include the West's provision of enormous financial and technical aid to Moscow. The Soviet president was not of a mind to defend Saddam Hussein's Kuwaiti adventure, especially inasmuch as such action would destroy his relations with the West and the United States, relations that had assumed strategic importance.

As Saddam Hussein's complex mind became increasingly convinced of the need to invade Kuwait to extricate Iraq from its economic problems, it conditioned him, hour after hour and day after day, to perceive this invasion as a legitimate defensive initiative forced upon him. The Gulf countries refused to grant Saddam Hussein the 'strategic outlook' on the Gulf which he had requested, which included Warbah Island, Bubiyan Island, and other military bases in unspecified areas. Saddam Hussein coveted this outlook for psychological reasons (it would confirm Iraq's political leadership) and for strategic reasons (it would entrench Iraq as the protector of the Gulf and the largest military power on it). Saddam Hussein perceived this refusal as part of an American conspiracy to isolate Iraq from the Gulf (which explains his repeated, vehement statements against the American military presence in the Gulf, when this presence did not exceed several warships that had been in the Gulf for many years). When the American media began to escalate their criticism of the Iraqi president, and when voices were raised in the American House of Representatives and Senate calling for an economic boycott against Iraq, the Iraqi president interpreted these developments as a part of the same American conspiracy. When the Western countries were alerted to the size of Iraq's nuclear programme and took measures to counter it, Saddam Hussein believed he was seeing the final link in a conspiracy being waged against him. When the well-known Soviet expert, Primakov, subsequently stated that the Iraqi president believed that the entire world was 'engaged in a complex conspiracy to get rid of him', he was neither exaggerating nor mistaken.

All of these factors circulated in the mind of Saddam Hussein, making his decision to invade a preordained and inevitable destiny. It is in this context that we should interpret the remarks he made in a meeting which he held with a number of his senior officers in Kuwait in November 1990. Saddam Hussein then said that the decision to invade was the only decision in his life which he himself did not make, but rather, it was God the exalted and the sublime who made it directly!

2
THE STORM

Bodies of the dead
Were the only amulets
For that madness.

                    al-Mutanabbi

The occupation of Kuwait was carried out with rare effectiveness, which was acknowledged by Iraq's enemies as well as its friends. Chief among those who acknowledged the efficiency of the invasion were US Defense Department experts. Regardless of what has been said about Iraqi military superiority over Kuwait's military weakness, and whatever has been said about the 'surprise' and 'deception', there is no escaping the conclusion that the gaining of complete control over an entire state within the space of a few hours with limited losses was an impressive military achievement. This achievement highlights the fact that the occupation plan was executed masterfully and skilfully. The successful implementation of the detailed invasion plan suggests that the plan was based on continuous, real manoeuvres differing from ordinary military exercises. Thus, the decision to invade had to have been made long before the actual invasion. The available information does not permit us to determine precisely when the decision was made. However, we can assume that it was made at least a year before the invasion.

As the plan fermented in Saddam Hussein's mind and became for him a divinely ordained destiny, it only remained to prepare and select the appropriate moment to implement the decision. Many of the Iraqi president's actions and statements in the months preceding the invasion, which seemed extremely strange at the time, can now be understood without much trouble. As soon as Saddam Hussein made the decision to invade, the only thing that could have stopped him would have been enormous financial aid provided by the Gulf countries or substantial concessions by Kuwait that would have ended its independence. The Gulf states and Kuwait were unwilling to 'co-operate' in this regard.

In fairness to the truth, we should say that the Iraqi president 'hinted' at the gravity of the situation. He began to do so at the Amman summit held in early 1990. This was followed by many statements made by King Hussein and Yasir 'Arafat, which alluded to fears of approaching wars. Such signalling reached a peak at the Baghdad summit, which was held weeks before the invasion. However, this time the hint took the form of bitter sarcasm, when the Iraqi president told the amir of Kuwait, during this summit, that he would 'surprise him' with a visit to Kuwait, and that he would 'surprise him' with a comprehensive, final solution to the border issue. The Iraqi president must have laughed long that night as he recalled the warm welcome given by the amir to the two pleasant surprises. Disregarding the sarcasm, Saddam Hussein was amazed at the intense coldness, both insinuated and open, with which Gulf leaders received his requests.

The truth of the matter is that these leaders were intensely puzzled by the Iraqi president's behaviour following the end of his war with Iran. This war was a severe, terrifying ordeal that had endangered their countries and personal safety (the amir of Kuwait was miraculously saved from an assassination attempt planned by a group sympathetic to Iran). They had entered the ordeal on the side of the Iraqi president. They expected that a long period of stability and peace would prevail in the region after the war. They also expected their excellent relations with Iraq to continue. These leaders were surprised by the establishment of the Arab Co-operation Council. They, like others, learned about its establishment only when it was officially announced in the absence of any prior consultations with them. They could not understand the bond that united Iraq with a country such as Yemen or Jordan. The Gulf Co-operation Council had been established on the basis of geographical unity and tangible similarities in political systems, customs and traditions. The Arab Maghreb Union had also been established on the basis of a measure of social and geographical proximity. The Gulf leaders viewed the Arab Co-operation Council as a motley blend that had no justification. What troubled them most was this new Iraqi attitude. However, they did not permit their anxiety to lead them to believe that the final objective was the occupation of Kuwait.

The Gulf leaders were also surprised by the Iraqi leader's continuation and intensification of his armament programme. Nothing justified the Iraqi war arsenal that was growing daily. These leaders were perplexed by the Iraqi president's insistence on a military presence on the Gulf, especially after the strategic justification for such a presence was removed by the end of the Iranian–Iraqi war. The Gulf leaders' dismay was not allayed by the critical statements that had begun to come out of Baghdad regarding the American military presence in the Gulf, because these leaders knew for certain that Saddam Hussein had worked hard to lure the US navy into the tanker war and to involve it in a military confrontation with Iran.

The Gulf leaders were most baffled by Saddam Hussein's constant demands for more money. The Gulf's support of Iraq, in the view of these leaders, had been unprecedentedly generous in the history of Arab relations and of aid in general. Saddam Hussein's insistence on obtaining additional support following the war seemed incomprehensible to them. The Gulf was suffering from an enormous fall in oil prices. The price of a barrel of oil had dropped from $40 in the early 1980s and had stabilized in recent years at as little as $15 per barrel. In addition, there was a substantial drop in production levels. Everywhere in the Gulf government spending was declining, projects were being cut, and development was being affected. Bahrain and Oman were suffering from severe economic problems and the Kingdom of Saudi Arabia was being compelled to borrow domestically year after year to cover its budget deficit. In the United Arab Emirates, financial troubles caused a stoppage in the payment of salaries more than once. In Qatar, reserves dropped substantially. Therefore, Iraq's requests did not fall on deaf ears, as Saddam Hussein imagined, so much as on treasuries that were unable to respond positively.

The Gulf leaders did not understand the great controversy which Saddam Hussein had aroused regarding the oil production of Kuwait and Abu Dhabi. Disagreement over production levels had been an inseparable part of OPEC history. No two countries in the organization had not disagreed a number of times on production quotas and the manner of their distribution. Moreover, the subject of production quotas was constantly discussed and sometimes hotly disputed, even between Gulf countries. No one in the Gulf could understand the Iraqi president's claim that the Iraqi economy was being destroyed by a difference of a quarter of a million barrels per day in the production of Kuwait and Abu Dhabi, especially as it was clear that adherence to production quotas was, in reality, optional and subject to each country's discretion. The amount of excess production to which Iraq objected would have had no appreciable difference on price levels. The Gulf leaders believed that a difference of opinion over production could be settled, with patience or 'generosity of heart' according to the Gulf expression, as dozens of similar disputes had been settled previously. Herein lies another irony of the crisis: Saddam Hussein believed that Iraq was a victim of a plan that aimed to starve him, while Gulf leaders were dismayed by the Iraqi president's irritation over such a routine ordinary matter as production quotas!

Kuwait, with its reserves of approximately $100 billion, was the only Gulf state capable of providing additional, substantial support to Iraq. The Kuwaiti government was no doubt willing to provide such support in exchange for a final comprehensive settlement of the Iraqi–Kuwaiti border dispute and the removal of the sword hanging over Kuwait's head which threatened to drop at any moment. However, the Iraqi president did not offer any such settlement. This was not a matter of additional billions for Iraq. Rather, Kuwait was being asked to cancel Iraqi debts owed to it (close to $12 billion) and to compensate Iraq for the oil which Iraq claimed that Kuwait was taking from part of Iraq (the al-Rumaylah oil field) equivalent to about $2.4 billion. In addition, Iraq sought to lease the islands of Warbah and Bubiyan. On top of that, Iraq demanded an enormous, unspecified sum as the nucleus of an Arab Marshall Plan from which Iraq would benefit. In exchange, Iraq promised only to spare Kuwait until further notice. The Kuwaiti government viewed this situation as the epitome of extortion, which would mean the end of Kuwait as an independent state if it complied.

Hence, the debate raised over whether or not Saddam Hussein's threat to invade Kuwait was an unequivocal threat, as maintained by President Husni Mubarak, or a threat conditional on the success or failure of negotiations, as maintained by the Iraqi president, is almost irrelevant. As soon as Iraqi forces massed on the Kuwaiti border, nothing could have prevented an invasion except Kuwait's full capitulation to all Iraqi demands. This was what was in the mind of the Iraqi president, regardless of what he was saying. In the above-mentioned meeting with his officers in Kuwait in November 1990, Saddam Hussein stated that he was amazed when 'Izzat Ibrahim informed him, after returning from a meeting with the Kuwaiti crown prince in Jeddah, that Kuwait was not moving to save itself by responding favourably.

It is also clear to me that those who subsequently spoke of a lack of sufficient flexibility in the Kuwaiti position – I am referring specifically to King Hussein and Yasir 'Arafat – were both correct and incorrect. They were correct in maintaining that Kuwait did not display 'sufficient flexibility', because sufficient flexibility 'to stop the invasion' would have meant an immediate, unconditional capitulation to all Iraqi demands. They were incorrect if what they had in mind was 'flexibility' in its traditional sense, which is complete willingness to discuss all disputed matters without prior conditions. In this latter sense, the Kuwaitis showed the utmost flexibility. How could it be otherwise, with the fate of their country hanging in the balance?

Perhaps we can now ascertain the true facts about what occurred in the meeting between the Kuwaiti crown prince and the Iraqi vice president in Jeddah. The Kuwaiti delegation went equipped with instructions to examine every issue, while the Iraqi delegation went with instructions not to discuss anything, but only to accept capitulation. When it became clear to 'Izzat Ibrahim that Shaykh Sa'd al-'Abdallah al-Sabah did not intend to capitulate, he recommended postponing the discussion until the next meeting, which was to be held in Baghdad. He then excused himself from the meeting on the pretext of a headache.

Despite the warning signs, none of the Gulf leaders, even in their wildest dreams, expected that matters would actually end with the occupation of Kuwait. They preferred to seek any justification for Saddam Hussein's behaviour other than the true one and his goal as anything other than the true goal. They believed in the existence of red lines which no one would cross, not even Saddam Hussein. Their admiration for Saddam Hussein convinced them that it was impossible for him to 'betray' any one of them. They believed that their close personal connections with the Iraqi leader would guarantee the elimination of any accidental misunderstanding.

Kuwait did not declare a state of emergency. Nor did it call up its forces. Life in Kuwait continued at its normal pace. Even when Iraqi forces began to move, and the crown prince went to command headquarters to monitor the situation, he remained convinced that Iraqi forces would stop after crossing the border and not head toward the capital. He did not stir from his position until Iraqi forces came within sight of the capital. The next problem was convincing the amir, who had refused to move and would only agree to leave his palace as a result of intense pressure from the crown prince. The time between his departure and the arrival of Iraqi forces at the palace was a matter of minutes, not hours, so the extent to which Gulf rulers trusted Saddam Hussein now seems amazing and insane. Without understanding this blind trust, no one can comprehend the deep hatred that followed.

Perhaps no one in the entire world was more shocked by the invasion than King Fahd. The relationship between him and the Iraqi president went beyond friendship to real brotherly feeling. The two leaders met for the first time at the OPEC summit in Algeria in 1975. They immediately developed a friendship, as a result of which relations between the kingdom and Iraq became extremely warm following a long period of acute tension. Within a few months the two leaders were able to end the border dispute between the two countries, which had resisted all attempts to solve it over the years. Both leaders respected each other's ability to fulfill and honour their promises.

King Fahd was the only Gulf leader to whom the Iraqi president disclosed his intention to attack Iran. The king's advice was: 'I hope that you will hesitate, because war is easy to begin but difficult to end. I hope that you will think long before taking this step.' The Iraqi president's response was: 'I would rather die than hear these words from you. It did not occur to me that you were a coward.' The king responded: 'A coward is one who avoids telling the truth. I told you my opinion. You are more knowledgeable of your circumstances and conditions.' Two years after this exchange, Saddam Hussein acknowledged to the king that he was mistaken when he ignored his advice. The strange thing is that it is being written that the Saudis 'enticed' Saddam Hussein to attack Iran.

As soon as the war started, the kingdom's government threw all its weight behind Saddam Hussein. Not only was King Fahd Iraq's primary financier, he also urged that the other countries of the Gulf Co-operation Council provide every kind of aid to Iraq. The kingdom's assistance to Iraq included monetary gifts, oil loans, the transport of Iraqi oil to the Red Sea in a pipeline passing through Saudi territory, the financing of arms deals, intelligence co-operation, the provision of Iraq with information obtained by AWACS aircraft, the placing of Saudi ports and roads at the disposal of the Iraqi army, and the provision of food. King Fahd was convinced that the Iraqi president felt only deep gratitude to him and the kingdom. During the king's visit to Iraq, Saddam Hussein bestowed upon him the highest Iraqi decoration accompanied by elaborate public praise, which embarrassed the king.

Those who monitored Gulf radio and television broadcasts during the first days of the invasion of Kuwait noted with great amazement that these broadcasts made no mention of the invasion. The reason was simply that no one believed what had happened. The shock of the violence left Gulf governments paralysed. There was a consensus that there must have been a 'mistake' whose correction would restore things to normal. Until the matter was settled, it was thought preferable for Gulf radio and television stations to broadcast sentimental songs and literary talks, leaving news of the invasion to Radio Monte Carlo, CNN and the BBC.

When the shock wore off, Arab diplomacy became active at the highest levels in search of an Arab solution that would get the Iraqi army out of Kuwait. Every Arab leader and every foreign minister from the Atlantic Ocean to the Gulf was taking action. In every Arab capital, there were feverish contacts, continuous meetings, and the urgent exchange of delegations. A week after the invasion, the impossibility of arriving at a formula that would satisfy the two parties became clear. All that remained was to record positions in favour of or opposed to Iraq. This is exactly what happened at the Cairo emergency summit. Jordan, Yemen, the Palestine Liberation Organization,

Tunisia, Mauritania and Sudan sided with Iraq. Algeria was close to neutrality, despite its inclination toward Iraq. The other Arab countries lined up behind Kuwait, condemned the aggression, and welcomed the forces that were coming to repel it.

Would an 'Arab solution' have prevented the internationalization of the conflict? Would it have been able, if given a chance, to succeed as many said repeatedly during the conflict, with the chief among them, as before, King Hussein and Yasir 'Arafat? The truth of the matter, disregarding the claims and counterclaims, is that there was no single Arab solution but, from the start, two separate Arab solutions. The first solution included a formula that could have obtained the agreement of the Iraqi president and led to withdrawal of the Iraqi army. The essence of this formula was the removal of the al-Sabah family and the installation of a puppet government that would respond positively to all of Iraq's demands. This was actually the spirit of the Arab solution which King Hussein and Yasir 'Arafat were pursuing, whatever its legal structure and wording. Had it been possible to obtain such a solution, the crisis would have ended with Iraq's withdrawal. I would also go so far as to say that had Saddam Hussein been able to install a puppet government that would have responded to all his demands, he would have left Kuwait even without an Arab solution!

Those who adopted this solution after the invasion of Kuwait are the same persons who demanded 'adequate flexibility' from Kuwait before the invasion. In both instances, Kuwait was being asked to capitulate to all Iraqi demands (to which was added the removal of the ruling family after the invasion). Perhaps those who called for this solution were convinced that the situation would naturally be different after the invasion, so that it would be possible for an Arab formula to incorporate the new reality. Hence, we can say that those who thought that their solution had been aborted were true to themselves and their solution.

The second Arab solution was that adopted by Kuwait and its friends. It was based on the unconditional withdrawal of the Iraqi army and the return of the legitimate government. Those who expected Iraq to agree to this solution were undoubtedly over-optimistic. What would compel the victorious Iraqi president to undertake an unconditional withdrawal after he had achieved an unprecedented success in occupying Kuwait within a few hours? Saddam Hussein, who had undertaken the greatest adventure of his life and who had seized the prize, was not about to give it up out of respect for such an Arab solution.

Much has been written and will be written about what happened during the first week of the crisis: the contacts, the bilateral meetings, the mini-summit that was planned and then cancelled, and the emergency summit in Cairo. All those who participated in these historic events have had their say. Each party described the facts as it saw them and defended its viewpoint. This process will no doubt continue in the future. Although we could write large volumes recording all that happened in the greatest detail, we would ultimately discover that everything that happened in the first decisive week could be summarized in one sentence: the Iraqi president was only willing to leave Kuwait on his terms, and Kuwait and its allies were unwilling to accept these terms.

Some stated subsequently that they opposed Iraq's invasion of Kuwait, and that their position did not change until after the arrival of foreign forces in the Gulf. This statement might be true regarding the positions of individuals, groups, or parties, but it does not apply to governments. The truth, which is difficult for anybody to deny, is that in the first hours after the invasion there were governments that strongly opposed the invasion and governments that inclined toward sympathizing with it, even before the first foreign soldier set foot on Gulf soil. The real problem was not that an Arab solution did not exist. The problem was that the Arabs were not united in adopting a single solution. From the outset, there were Arab blocs, each with its own solution. Ultimately, neither of the two solutions settled the problem!

While these events were occurring in the Arab world, Western capitals were receiving the news of the invasion with almost as much astonishment as the Gulf capitals. There had been whispered warnings at low levels in Western intelligence agencies. However, it seems certain, from information that has since come to light, that no Western head of state was given a clear warning of the imminence of the invasion. This seems difficult to believe given the capacity of Western intelligence, which can eavesdrop on a telephone conversation anywhere in the world and can photograph an apple on a tree from far out in space. The irony is that sophisticated technology can convey information but cannot reveal intentions. The Iraqi military concentration on the Kuwaiti border was no secret requiring satellite detection. The secret was the intention to invade. It must be acknowledged that the Iraqi president clearly succeeded in concealing this intention from all human and electronic spies.

From the many reports and studies which have appeared that provide a day-by-day account of what occurred in US decision-making agencies, we have an almost complete picture of the general outline of the American decision. The American president hastened to freeze Iraqi and Kuwaiti funds in American banks. He ordered the State Department to begin a campaign to condemn the invasion inside and outside the United Nations. He spent long hours on the telephone in an attempt to mobilize an alliance to counter the invasion. The American president asked his cabinet for specific options. Apparently no plan existed for responding to an invasion scenario. The rapid deployment plan that had been formulated to repel a Soviet attack on the Gulf was the only well studied military option. The president ordered the immediate implementation of the plan with the necessary changes to suit the circumstances of the Iraqi invasion. The intentions of the American president were clear from the outset, namely, not to permit this invasion to succeed. This position did not change at all.

Recent reports and studies indicate that the American president was the only 'hawk' among a group of 'doves', which included the secretary of state, the secretary of defense and the chief of staff (the president's aides in the White House were, as expected, supportive of their boss). We should note here that all American agencies participating in the decision-making process agreed that the US national interest could not permit Saddam Hussein to control a quarter of the world's oil directly or indirectly, and that this interest consequently required removing him from Kuwait. The only disagreement between the 'hawk' and the 'doves' related to the means. Senior administration officials believed that economic sanctions, especially prohibiting Iraq from selling its oil, would so weaken Iraq as to force Saddam Hussein to abandon Kuwait.

The American president was convinced that there was not enough time to wait until sanctions had the desired effect. He was convinced that a direct military confrontation had become necessary. Hence his daily insistence on 'specific options', which included first a defensive plan and then a plan for attack.

Following the Vietnam war, the American military establishment had become convinced that a repetition of what happened there had to be avoided. The military intervention in Vietnam began with a limited number of forces, which then increased gradually as the conflict escalated, in the absence of a clear strategic objective from the outset. Over the years a conviction developed that the United States must not intervene militarily anywhere unless such intervention was dictated by the national interest and was accompanied by a clear objective and adequate forces. Accordingly, symbolic military measures, such as air and naval raids, were excluded as options. The first batch of forces totalled close to a quarter of a million soldiers. When this number was in place, the American president decided to double it.

Historians will deal at length with the moment at which the American president made his final decision to use force. Was it during the week of Christmas December 1990, as some observers maintain? Or was it several days before the start of the air assault on 17 January 1991, as other observers maintain? I am inclined toward placing the 'actual' decision, which is more important than the 'final' decision, at the time when the president decided to give American forces an offensive capability by doubling their number in the first week of November 1990. After the United States had decided to dispatch half a million soldiers, it was impossible to retreat from the edge of the abyss.

Unfortunately for the Iraqi president, and fortunately for Kuwait, the man living in the White House during the invasion was George Bush. Bush came to the presidency with extensive experience in international affairs, which an American president rarely possesses at the start of his tenure. Bush had been a member of Congress, a US ambassador to the United Nations, a US ambassador to China, the head of the Central Intelligence Agency, and vice president for two consecutive

terms.[1] Before entering politics, he was active in the oil indus-
try in Texas. Thus, the strategic dimensions of the invasion of
Kuwait were clearer in his mind than would have been the
case with any of his predecessors in the presidency (or any of
his senior aides).

When Kuwait fell under Saddam Hussein's grip, all Gulf oil,
at least in terms of production and pricing, was at the mercy
of the Iraqi president, who could threaten the industrialized
world as much as he wanted. Moreover, the fall of Kuwait
made the independence of the other Gulf countries dependent
on the whims of the Iraqi president, who could repeat the
'lesson' to his heart's content.

In addition to strategic calculations, the scenes of the
invasion on American television aroused feelings of anger and
disgust. The American people, like any other people, were
sympathetic to the small victim of a giant adversary (hence
Israel has always tried to present itself, erroneously, as a brave
little girl surrounded by merciless ogres!). The American president was able to depict his position as the defence of the
freedom and independence of small peoples and the new international order. If it is true that the strategic calculations that
compelled him to counter the Iraqi invasion would oblige him
to disregard the invasion of countries like Somalia or Djibouti,
it is also true that the feelings of revulsion generated by the
invasion enabled the American president to enhance his position with a shining display of idealism. Adherence to principles
no doubt becomes easy when these principles correspond with
the national interest.

If the invasion constituted the greatest crisis in the American
president's life, King Fahd Bin ʿAbd al-ʿAziz, for his part, was
also experiencing his most difficult and trying days. The king
was approaching 70, and he felt that he had had his share of
problems. He was looking forward to spending the rest of his
rule in peace and quiet. The king received training in foreign
policy when he was an adolescent at the side of his legendary
father, and he experienced its sudden crises and pitfalls during
the days of his two brothers, King Saʿud and King Faysal. He
then became the actual formulator of Saudi policy when he
became King Khalid's heir apparent in 1975. King Fahd is by

[1]Compare these qualifications to the qualifications of Kennedy, Johnson, Ford,
Carter and Reagan at the start of their tenures.

nature pacific, to an extent bordering on meekness. He is cautious to the point of hesitation, and he has learned from long experience to view matters realistically and practically. He has always criticized heads of state who aspire to roles that transcend their capability and that of their countries. Some of his critics view his foreign policy as no more than 'chequebook diplomacy'. However, if the chequebook has played a clear role in his foreign policy, he also has the ability to calm an explosive situation, and the rare gift of persuading others while realistically evaluating his own capabilities and those of others. The king's main foreign policy objective is for himself and his kingdom to be left in peace.

Because of the invasion of Kuwait, the king found himself compelled to confront two options, both of them chilling. The first option was to leave Kuwait to its destiny and to protect, in the short term in any case, the well-being of the kingdom from troubles. The second option was to oppose the occupation of Kuwait and subject his country to the dangers of war, which he was keen to avoid at any cost. He could not allow Kuwait to perish, given the strong relations between the two countries. As a person, he could not forget that his grandfather and father, when they were exiled from Najd, which was under the control of the Rashid family, had found refuge with the al-Sabah family in Kuwait. However, the king was realistic. He realized that a military confrontation with Iraq would be certain suicide. The king had always rejected an American military presence in his country. He realized the implications of such a presence, not only for public opinion abroad, but also for domestic public opinion. He continued to weigh matters. When it became clear that no Arab solution would remove the occupier from Kuwait, and when he received reports confirming the massing of a large number of Iraqi tanks near the Saudi border, he decided that the situation could no longer allow delay, and he consented to the arrival of American forces.

Some have subsequently maintained that Iraqi forces had taken a defensive posture, and that there was no clear intention to invade the kingdom. Such an assertion might be correct. However, after what had happened in Kuwait – after what had been thought impossible had taken place – the king was unwilling to place himself at the mercy of Saddam Hussein.

Gone was the time when Saddam Hussein's promises, were accepted for what they were. Intense suspicion replaced the old absolute trust.

Anyone who reaches a decision quickly, or based on a fleeting sentiment, can change that decision with equal speed and with a mere change of heart. On the other hand, anyone who reaches a decision after painful heart-searching is likely to find it especially difficult to go back on that decision. After the king made his decision, there was absolutely no possibility of retreating from it. Once the battle began, it could not end until Kuwait's liberation. All of Saddam Hussein's abuse directed personally against the king and all of the Iraqi president's threats about using missiles and gas and the rivers of blood that would flow failed to change the king's position. Those who are close to Fahd Bin 'Abd al-'Aziz know that stubbornness is no less an important feature of his psychological make-up than peacefulness or caution. This was the aspect which Saddam Hussein could not read. Saddam Hussein attempted, shortly before the air war, to meet with King Fahd personally. All of the messages sent by Saddam Hussein to King Fahd through various indirect channels emphasized that the problem would be solved if this meeting took place. However, the king always refused to meet with him unless Saddam Hussein officially declared his resolve to withdraw from Kuwait.

Because of the fateful decisions made by the American president and the Saudi king, the success of the Iraqi invasion became doubtful. However, the failure of the adventure seemed certain once it became clear that the Soviet Union, while preferring not to resort to force, did not oppose it, and that the five permanent members of the Security Council were in complete agreement on the need to oppose the invasion. With the final warning and the vote in the US Senate and House of Representatives in favour of the use of force, the only remaining question concerned the price that would have to be paid to dislodge the Iraqi army.

During this time, Saddam Hussein's plans were changing from day to day. His basic plan was clearly to install a puppet Kuwaiti government that would profess absolute loyalty to him (i.e., fulfil all of his demands), thereby permitting him to withdraw his forces and depict the entire operation as a response to a call made by the legitimate Kuwaiti government.

This is the reason that compelled Saddam Hussein to condition his exit from Kuwait on there being no Arab condemnation. Otherwise, the operation would become an invasion, and the illusion of legitimate intervention would evaporate. When it became clear to the Iraqi president that he would not find any well known Kuwaiti to co-operate with him, he attempted to form a phantom government comprising a number of junior Kuwaiti and Iraqi officers unknown to anyone. The 'government' was an object of ridicule that aroused the derision of enemies and the dismay of friends. In the face of Arab opposition, which his allies were unable to neutralize, and growing international opposition, Saddam Hussein decided to call things by their real name. The idea of 'Unification' was born, and Kuwait became the nineteenth province of Iraq.

The big question that puzzled observers throughout the crisis, and which continues to puzzle them now and will surely occupy researchers in the future, is: Why did Saddam Hussein remain in Kuwait when it became clear that an easy act of piracy was turning into a fatal trap? Why did he not cut his losses and withdraw, especially when the door was opened to an honourable withdrawal through a number of initiatives, the most important being the French and Soviet?

I do not claim to possess the answer to this question. However, I maintain that the answer should be sought by examining the nature of Saddam Hussein's decision to embark on the Kuwait adventure and the psyche of the Iraqi president. Embarking on an adventure is not a routine decision which is made after quiet, objective calculations. Nor is it a decision which can be reversed as soon as all or some of the calculations prove to be mistaken. An adventure is a desperate action in which one wagers everything on a specific result and then has only to wait for the result. A gambler who bets everything he has on a specific horse would be unlikely to retreat from his choice, if it were possible, at the start of the race. A gambler who enters a casino and bets his entire savings on a specific number on the roulette wheel can only stand helpless, waiting for the wheel to stop. After Saddam Hussein bet on the Kuwaiti adventure, it was impossible for him to retreat before the final result.

We find the second part of the answer in the nature of Saddam Hussein, who is able to transform any adventure into a legitimate act of self-defence and then into an inescapable 'fate'. Belief in historical destiny is apparently a characteristic of all 'historic' leaders. For example, Albert Speer, who was Hitler's architect and then minister of war industries, told me that the German leader, despite his lack of religious faith, which he did not conceal, and his scorn for all religions, had an unshakeable belief in his historical destiny. Even when defeat became patently clear, Hitler remained convinced that the fate that had selected him to resurrect and lead the German nation would inevitably intervene again, miraculously, to change the course of events. He maintained this strange belief until his final days. There is no doubt that Saddam Hussein, regardless of his religious belief or lack of it, believes in his historical destiny, and that this destiny will intervene at the appropriate time to decide the conflict in his favour. Saddam Hussein did not exaggerate when he told a CNN correspondent in Baghdad, as the air war was at its peak, that he had not the slightest doubt as to his ultimate victory. In a press interview with an American newspaper after the war, Tarik 'Aziz acknowledged that the Iraqi leadership was 'fatalistic'.

However, Saddam Hussein's surrender to his fate was neither passive nor weak. He turned Kuwait into the largest battlefield since the Second World War, where he massed half a million soldiers. He took many measures: he held foreign hostages in an attempt to prevent an attack before the completion of his preparations; he planted explosives in all the oil wells in Kuwait and threatened to detonate them at the start of any attack; and he took measures to pollute the whole Gulf by pumping oil into it. The land borders were transformed into 'killing fields'. If the attacker escaped the mines, he would be buried by artillery. If he escaped from artillery, he would fall into the burning trenches.

Saddam Hussein's plan was the height of simplicity (he has stated more than once that a complicated problem can only be confronted with simple measures). The plan was based on absorbing the air strike and waiting for the 'mother of battles' on the ground. The 'killing fields' would ensure the loss of thousands of American soldiers, which would mean that the United States had lost the battle. The plan in itself was not foolish. The problem was that it lacked the technology needed for success.

Dozens, perhaps hundreds, of books will be written about 'Desert Storm'. Military experts will study what happened in great detail. The military plan will become a part of the curriculum of war colleges everywhere in the world. However, I imagine that no one in the end will deny that the situation can be summarized as follows: the battle ended as it did because it was between two armies, one of which was fighting the last battle of the First World War, and the other waging the first battle of the Third World War!

3

COALITION AND COUNTER-COALITION

So many tongues and so many nations and so many translators.

al-Mutanabbi

A long time will pass before Gulf leaders and ordinary people in the Gulf will understand the reasons that motivated a number of Arab leaders to support the Iraqi invasion of Kuwait. The prevailing theory at present is that of collusion. According to this theory, the invasion plan was arranged in advance between the Iraqi president and his allies, who supported him in exchange for a known share of the booty. The truth is that no one possesses absolute proof of the accuracy of this theory. It is in the nature of collusion that it is neither recorded nor documented in a way that would allow it to be proved. Until irrefutable evidence emerges, collusion will remain a mere hypothesis, and it will be as difficult to prove it as it will be to convince those who believe it to abandon it.

While collusion is difficult to prove, some of the considerations underlying a number of leaders' support for the Iraqi president can certainly be inferred without much trouble. There apparently was a feeling among these leaders that their support for Saddam Hussein would not destroy their links with the Gulf. This feeling was expressed on more than one occasion by Yasir ʿArafat during the crisis. He emphasized that the current schism was no different from schisms in the past, and that it would end at the appropriate time, just as previous schisms had ended. This feeling stems from the experience of the past, when the expression 'God has forgiven the past' was sufficient grounds for forgetting any dispute and opening a new chapter. The ruling regimes in the Gulf possess neither revolutionary ideologies that justify violence, nor party apparatuses capable of taking the offensive, nor news media that are used to propaganda skirmishes. They have always been

45

willing to make peace with those who attack them as soon as such attackers displayed a desire to make peace. None of the invasion's supporters thought that matters would be any different this time around.

Confidence in their ability to regain the favour of the Gulf countries when necessary convinced them that political support of the invasion would have no serious consequences. There was another consideration working in the opposite direction, namely, the danger of opposing Saddam Hussein in the greatest adventure of his life. We can mention in this regard that two prominent Palestinian leaders, Abu Iyyad and Abu Hawl, were killed by their personal bodyguards as they were drafting a communiqué in which they condemned Palestinian involvement in the Kuwaiti adventure. If the suspicious circumstances of the assassination do not allow us to be certain of the identity of the killer, they give us a very clear idea of his motives. It was an open secret in Palestinian circles that the private plane of Yasir ʿArafat was Iraqi, that its entire crew was Iraqi, and that the Iraqi president was closely linked with a number of persons who surround Palestinian leaders.

However, we must now leave these considerations aside and attempt to place ourselves in the decision-maker's shoes. We will begin with that man whose position caused the greatest astonishment, displeasure, and bitterness in the Gulf, namely Yasir ʿArafat. There is no doubt that the PLO chairman, like all Palestinians, began to experience deep and growing frustration as he watched the years pass without any significant progress for the Palestinian cause. On the contrary, it was suffering setbacks. He tried violence, but that resulted in worldwide condemnation of terrorism and led to an impasse. He bowed to pressure to pursue a peaceful solution by officially renouncing the use of violence and declaring his willingness to recognize Israel's right to exist and to co-exist with it. In exchange for this historic concession, he was faced with only contempt from the Israelis and coldness from the Americans, while there was absolute silence in the Arab world. It seemed to Yasir ʿArafat that the Palestinian cause was dying a slow death, and no one was intervening to save it.

Arab conditions, in the Palestinian leader's view, did not call for optimism. The PLO's bridges with Syria had been destroyed, and there was no real hope of restoring them. Yasir

'Arafat believed that Egypt, with its continued adherence to the Camp David agreement, had given all that it could. He decided that the Gulf countries could do nothing for the cause except urge the United States, with words alone, to seek a peaceful solution and provide financial assistance, which had begun to decline. Yasir 'Arafat became convinced that relying on the moderate regimes would do nothing to advance the Palestinian cause.

At this time, his relations with the Iraqi president were becoming closer and warmer. Iraq was a strong fortress with close to a million under arms and it had the largest arsenal in the region, which included various weapons of mass destruction. It seemed to Yasir 'Arafat that the placing of this enormous military force in the service of the Palestinian cause would necessarily lead to a break in the deadlock. If the price was the sacrificing of the ruling family in Kuwait, this seemed a reasonable exchange for the great gain to the cause.

This decision was not made quite freely. Years ago, the PLO had begun slowly and imperceptibly to surrender its power to Baghdad, due to a number of factors, including: the appearance of the long Israeli arm in Tunisia; the setbacks in Palestinian–Syrian relations; the pervasive lack of trust in Palestinian–Jordanian relations; the troubles in Lebanon; and the refusal of the Gulf countries to shelter Palestinian fighters and their weapons. With all of these factors coming into play, more and more Palestinian leaders, with their personnel and material, were settling in Baghdad, which became a second home for the Palestinian leader himself.

Yasir 'Arafat could not resist the temptation to benefit, as a Palestinian, from Saddam Hussein's Kuwaiti adventure, which appeared to the Palestinian leader as offering pure gain with no risk of major damage. If Saddam Hussein succeeded in holding on to Kuwait, the Palestinians would be the primary partner in the victory. If the war became protracted (in many public statements, Yasir 'Arafat estimated that the war would last for more than three years), the Palestinian cause would lose nothing and perhaps benefit. Even in the worst-case scenario, namely the complete collapse of the adventure, Yasir 'Arafat believed that the exit of the Iraqi army from Kuwait under pressure from the international community would permit him to demand that the international community exercise the same pressure on Israel.

Hence, this writer believes that it is inaccurate to speak of Yasir 'Arafat's support of Saddam Hussein's Kuwaiti adventure. It is more accurate to speak of Yasir 'Arafat's attempt to exploit Saddam Hussein's Kuwaiti adventure by endorsing it in the interest of the Palestinian cause (as he saw it). Proof of this claim may be the fact that the linking of Kuwait with Palestine did not originate in the Iraqi leader's mind. Nor was it in his calculations. The idea originated with the Palestinian leader, as he himself stated publicly on more than one occasion. The Iraqi president adopted it as an effective weapon in his media war. The idea of a linkage between the Kuwaiti problem and the Palestinian problem did not appear in any Iraqi official or media statements until ten days after the invasion had begun.

These then are the calculations of the Palestinian leader. They are entirely Palestinian calculations with no connection whatsoever with Kuwait or its fate. Yasir 'Arafat was assisted in adopting this policy by the strong Palestinian support for Saddam Hussein which he saw being unleashed by the Iraqi leader's famous statement about 'burning half of Israel'. The Palestinians viewed this as the first time since the days of the late President Jamal 'Abd al-Nasir of Egypt that an Arab leader was emerging to challenge Israel militarily in an outspoken, public manner. Moreover, the new knight's chances of success seemed much better than those of the old. Saddam Hussein was supported by a huge army with eight years of bitter combat experience, thousands of tanks, hundreds of aircraft, an unknown number of missiles, and strange weapons, which no one could be sure were chemical, biological or nuclear, and which could 'burn half of Israel'. It was to be expected that the Palestinians would go out into the streets to pledge their 'spirit and blood' to Saddam Hussein. It would have been strange had they not done so.[1]

At the same time, Yasir 'Arafat's position seemed astonishing, and suicidal to the point of being incomprehensible to

[1] How could the ordinary Palestinian or Arab know that, while Saddam Hussein was making these fiery statements, he was concurrently asking Prince Bandar Bin Sultan, the Saudi ambassador in Washington, to inform the American government not to take these statements seriously?!

Gulf leaders, who still fail to understand it. Every Kuwaiti child knows that Kuwait welcomed Yasir 'Arafat when he was a young engineer. In Kuwait, the young engineer became, by his own admission, a millionaire. Fatah was started in Kuwait. The Kuwaitis were completely perplexed by the hostile behaviour of a man towards whom Kuwait had been so generous. Kuwait had opened its doors to close to 400,000 Palestinians, who, regardless of what is said about their being treated as second-class persons, worked in Kuwait and sent a portion of their income to their families in the occupied territories and a portion to support the PLO. The 'Palestinian lobby' almost managed Kuwait's Arab policy. The Kuwaiti government's sensitivity toward any issue harmful to the Palestinians was well known. The Kuwaiti government hastened to suspend aid to Jordan following tension in Jordanian–Palestinian relations. It froze its relations with the Syrian government following tension in Palestinian–Syrian relations. More than one American observer has pointed out, correctly, that the Kuwaiti government has voted almost regularly against American positions in the United Nations and the Kuwaiti government's alignment with the Palestinian cause, is the most important reason.[1] The Gulf provided continuous, regular financial support to the PLO. The Gulf media always took a positive position on the PLO. This position did not change over the years (the Gulf always aligned itself with the Palestinians in every dispute). The Palestinian uprising in the occupied territories reverberated in the Gulf press as it did in no other press in the Arab world.

King Fahd Bin 'Abd al-'Aziz, in particular, was strongly disappointed with Yasir 'Arafat's behaviour, because the king had given him and his cause what no other Arab head of state had given. Fahd Bin 'Abd al-'Aziz was crown prince when he managed to convince President Carter to recognize the PLO officially in exchange for the PLO's recognition of Resolutions 242 and 338 (without the need to recognize Israel and with the right to maintain reservations regarding parts of the two

[1]It was no coincidence that the meeting between the PLO representative and the American ambassador to the United Nations during President Carter's tenure, Andrew Young, took place at the home of the Kuwaiti ambassador to the United Nations at the time, 'Abdallah Bisharah. The meeting provoked retaliation on the part of the Zionist lobby, and the American ambassador was forced to resign.

resolutions). This was a major victory for the cause by any measure. Yasir 'Arafat could not believe his ears when he heard the 'good news'. He informed the crown prince of his consent to the initiative and asked to be given two days to consult with his comrades in the leadership. After several days, instead of approval for the initiative, the Palestinian leadership sent a long list of questions and requests for clarifications. The Saudi crown prince could only inform the person who brought the list that he could present it to the American ambassador in Beirut. At this time, news of the Carter initiative began to leak and it was attacked strongly by the Zionist lobby. The American president was compelled to retreat. The king strongly believed, and continues to believe, that the Palestinian leadership lost an historic opportunity that will not be repeated.

The second personal initiative undertaken by the king in the interest of the Palestinian cause – we should mention here that the king, by nature, eschews personal initiatives – is what became known as the 'Fahd peace plan'. The similarity between this plan and official Palestinian positions gave rise to a firm belief among many at the time that the plan had been formulated by people inside Fatah. The plan provided for the establishment of a Palestinian state with Jerusalem as its capital, the implementation of all UN resolutions regarding Palestine, and the Security Council's formulation of the necessary arrangements for the peaceful coexistence of all countries in the region. The plan contained no stipulation for the recognition of Israel or the establishment of diplomatic relations with it. It began as a press statement. Shortly thereafter, it came to enjoy growing support in the Arab world and then in different countries in Asia, Africa and Europe. It was then officially approved at the Fez summit in 1982. The king was extremely dismayed when he saw the Palestinian leadership beginning to criticize the plan instead of adopting and promoting it. One of the ironies was that the Palestinian leadership ignored the plan because they considered it an 'American plan', even though the United States clearly opposed it.

During the Israeli invasion of Lebanon, the invading forces surrounded Beirut, where Yasir 'Arafat and a number of resistance fighters were located. The Israeli government intended to solve its problem with the PLO in a radical way by finishing

50

off Yasir ʿArafat and his comrades. The Palestinian leader sent call after call to the Arab countries. He received a cable from Colonel Muʿammar al-Qaddafi advising him and his comrades to die as martyrs to ensure their entry into history. The rest of the Arab capitals remained silent (perhaps some of them were whispering 'You have only yourselves to blame'). King Fahd took command and began immediately to pressure the United States to force Israel to abandon its plan to enter Beirut and destroy the Palestinian resistance. Purely by coincidence, I had the opportunity to hear what King Fahd said to the American President Ronald Reagan, because I was assisting in translation. I can only express my belief that the king's position is what saved the Palestinian leader from a tragic fate. President Reagan, in his memoirs, refers to this telephone call, stating that immediately after the conversation he contacted Israeli Prime Minister Begin and asked him not to enter Beirut. Israeli forces stopped on the heights overlooking the Lebanese capital and Yasir ʿArafat and his comrades were able subsequently to leave Beirut by sea as heroes. The touching cable which the Palestinian leader sent to the king leaves no doubt that Yasir ʿArafat knew at the time that he was indebted to the king for his life and the lives of his comrades.

The truth of the matter is that Palestinian support of the invasion of Kuwait cannot be understood without taking into account the emotional, excitable aspect of Yasir ʿArafat's personality. I have observed this trait on numerous occasions. I mean no disparagement or criticism. This trait is probably among the reasons for his success in retaining the leadership of the Palestinian movement. I still remember, after King Faysal's assassination in 1975, that I saw Yasir ʿArafat wailing like an old, bereaved peasant woman, hitting the walls as he walked, while the sons and brothers of King Faysal were receiving condolences with calm and dignity. I still remember the day in the 1970s when I was receiving an official guest at Riyadh Airport. I heard a large commotion and I thought that a fight had broken out. When I moved closer, I found that the source of the commotion was Yasir ʿArafat, who was explaining to those receiving him the secrets of the Palestinian–Syrian crisis in a voice that could be heard outside the terminal. Those who have witnessed Yasir ʿArafat at successive Arab summits have been amazed at his outstanding ability to shake and weep while talking about his friends (or his enemies). They are likewise amazed at his outstanding ability to turn friends into enemies (and vice versa!).

Thus Yasir ʿArafat believed that he was serving the Palestinian cause by supporting the invasion of Kuwait, whereas Gulf public opinion believed that the Palestinian cause was as good as finished in the light of the Palestinian leader's position. The essence of the Palestinian cause is based on a moral/legal principle, namely the right to self-determination, on the basis of which the Palestinians are demanding an independent Palestinian state. Disregarding the Palestinian leader's motives and objectives, the Palestinian leadership's welcoming of the liquidation of an existing, independent state, Kuwait, no doubt weakens the moral basis of its own demands for a state.

An explanation of the Jordanian position does not raise the same problems as the Palestinian position. King Hussein assumed power at an early age. He has faced troubles and crises which no other contemporary head of state has faced. It is no coincidence that the king borrows, for his memoirs (the English edition) a passage from Shakespeare: 'Uneasy lies the head that wears the crown' (Henry IV, Part 2)! The king has been able to remain on the throne without a party or powerful tribe to support him, and without a rich treasury. He does so by relying mainly on his extraordinary ability to manoeuvre and, in particular, his ability to see approaching storms and move with them until they can be faced at the appropriate moment.

During the Nasirist tide, King Hussein was ahead of the tide. He dismissed Glubb Pasha (the commander-in-chief of the Jordanian armed forces), co-operated with the Nasirist government of Sulayman al-Nabulsi, then turned against the Nasirist current. Without a truce followed by a sudden onslaught, it is doubtful whether the king would have been able to retain his throne. Before the June 1967 war, the Jordanian king was among the few who predicted its coming shock. The king forgot his long, bitter history with the Egyptian President, Jamal ʿAbd al-Nasir and threw himself into his embrace shortly before the battle. Following the war, Jordan became a Palestinian territory. Members of the Palestinian resistance were directing traffic in the streets of Amman, and aircraft were being hijacked, brought down in Jordanian territory, and then destroyed without the knowledge of the Jordanian government. King Hussein remained patient until matters reached a climax. Then came the bloody confrontation which entered history as Black September. Yasir 'Arafat would have been killed in Amman had it not been for the intervention of a delegation sent by the Arab summit that had convened in Cairo at the time. It is one of the ironies of fate that the delegation member who was able to smuggle Yasir 'Arafat through Jordanian lines was none other than the current crown prince of Kuwait, Shaykh Sa'd al-'Abdallah al-Sabah!

'Going along' with the Iraqi invasion of Kuwait was thus consistent with King Hussein's style of dealing with dangerous crises threatening his throne (he knows better than anyone else what threatens the throne which he has held for close to 40 years!). In 1989, demonstrations occurred in Jordan protesting against unemployment caused by the economic recession and during the disturbances acts of violence occurred in a number of Jordanian cities. As is his custom, the king rode on the wave of the future, which this time was democracy. He announced free elections. The Islamic 'fundamentalist' movement in Jordan was the only movement that enjoyed the sympathy of the Jordanian government (a sympathy the government has used as a card in its dispute with Syria). When elections were held, this movement was the only organized party in Jordan, which was able to act effectively. It is no wonder that it obtained a quarter of the seats in the Jordanian parliament.

In addition to the king's careful calculations, an effective lobby in the parliament was pushing Jordan toward Iraq. Above all, the Jordanian media was wholly sympathetic to the Iraqi leader, and it mobilized a large sector of public opinion in support of him. Because the majority of Jordanian people, who are Palestinians, were enthusiastic about Saddam Hussein, King Hussein was not harmonizing his position with his narrow interests alone, but with the majority of public opinion in his country.

The Jordanian king also felt some deep bitterness toward some of the actions of the Gulf countries. He believed that the aid given to Jordan was much less than Jordan deserved. In the king's opinion, the abandonment by some Gulf countries of their aid commitments was responsible for the disturbances in Jordanian cities. Also, the fact that he was compelled from time to time to tour the Gulf to solicit more aid insulted both his personal honour and that of Jordan.[1]

However, none of these considerations convinced the Gulf leaders. None of them could understand how the moderate king could suddenly become an extremist radical. None of them understood how the West's premier ally in the Arab region had become an enemy of foreign intervention (no Gulf official has forgotten that King Hussein was the first Arab head of state to summon British forces to protect him in the 1950s). Regarding the matter of Gulf aid for Jordan, Gulf leaders believed that they had fulfilled their commitments to Jordan commendably. Their actions were restricted by the recession that was affecting the Gulf as much as Jordan. Some of the king's demands seemed extremely odd. One Gulf official remarked: 'Is it not strange for King Hussein to ask us to equip his army with modern fighters when he sees that we have not even purchased such fighters for our own army?!'

If Yasir ʿArafat's tendency to impetuosity and excitability, and King Hussein's history of conciliation alternating with confrontation render their positions on the Gulf crisis somewhat understandable, there was nothing to forecast the Yemeni position. President ʿAli ʿAbdallah Salih enjoyed extensive Saudi support, which made him, in the eyes of his rivals in Yemen, a 'Saudi protégé' or 'the Saudis' man' (we leave it to psychologists to determine the effect of these descriptions on his position during the crisis). There were hundreds of thousands of Yemeni citizens working in the kingdom. They were not subject to any visa or residency requirements, nor did they have to obtain work permits. For all practical purposes, this meant that they were treated like Saudis, unlike other Arab and Islamic immigrant communities in Saudi Arabia. Co-operation between the Saudi and Yemeni governments covered different political, economic, military, commercial, and cultural areas. The only visible problem between the two countries concerned the borders. Each of the two parties had concluded that it is preferable not to magnify the issue. In addition to Saudi aid,

---

[1]King Hussein told several of his visitors that when he explained to the amir of Kuwait the dimensions of the economic crisis in Jordan, the amir was content to say that Jordan, which is not an oil state, should expand its services and facilities.

Yemen received significant aid from Kuwait and Abu Dhabi. It occurred to no one, until the Gulf crisis, that the outward friendliness in Yemeni–Gulf relations masked a great deal of internal bitterness.

Yemeni decision-makers, however, viewed matters quite differently. Regardless of what is said about Gulf aid, this aid was insufficient. (We have seen this dilemma before and we will see it many times in the future; how much is sufficient?!) The restriction of the membership of the Gulf Co-operation Council to its six present members made it appear to Yemeni leaders that the council was a club for the rich, and that Yemen was excluded from it because it is poor. Strong internal factors inclined Yemen toward the Iraqi president in the absence of other balancing factors. Perhaps the background of the Yemeni decision to support Saddam Hussein can best be explained by reviewing the abundant sensitivities in Yemeni–Saudi relations.

First of all, there is the legacy of wariness and distrust which arose after the Yemeni revolution in September 1962. Saudi Arabia supported Yemeni royalists in their confrontation with the fledgling republic and the Egyptian forces that had come to assist it (the Saudi government viewed the republic as no more than a Nasirist conspiracy). The kingdom took this position for reasons related more to its conflict with President ʿAbd al-Nasir than to Yemen's domestic circumstances; although the kingdom abandoned its support of the royalists after the Egyptian army withdrew from Yemen in 1967, and the kingdom's relations with the republican government had been normalized then deepened, a residue of negative attitudes toward the kingdom has persisted in the minds of many Yemeni public opinion leaders. Yemeni intellectuals were convinced that the kingdom did not want Yemen to develop, progress and stabilize. (If Yemeni intellectuals were aware of King Fahd's opinion of Imam Ahmad's policies, they would be surprised to find that it does not differ much from their own – but that is another story!)

Given this legacy, the border problem assumed symbolic importance. Many of the Yemenis came to view the borders as a symbol of the hegemony of Saudi Arabia, which had stolen some Yemeni territory by force of arms. The Saudi government could not understand the Yemeni position, which was to reject recognition of borders that had been agreed officially and definitively in the al-Ta'if Treaty signed between the two countries in 1934. The border problem was a double-edged sword. Saudi insistence on translating the terms of the treaty into an actual demarcation on the ground showed, in Yemen's view, a determination to remind Yemenis of what they wished to forget, while the Yemeni government's procrastination in agreeing to demarcate the borders was, in the Saudi government's view, a sign of blatant insincerity.

In addition to these two problems, a third complication arose over the unification of the two parts of Yemen. Yemeni leaders thought that the kingdom opposed the unification of the two parts because of the threat posed by the combining of their forces. Such a belief was correct to some degree when South Yemen was a Marxist state and unification would have meant the transfer of the Marxist 'germs' from the South to the North. With the collapse of the Marxist regime in South Yemen and the bankruptcy of Marxism everywhere, it was no longer important to the kingdom whether or not the two parts united. If there was any opposition to the unification, it remained only a matter of feeling. What is certain is that the kingdom would undertake no measure of any type to impede the unification.

The fourth complication is the sensitivity of the poor neighbour *vis-à-vis* the rich neighbour (and vice versa!).[1] While the kingdom has regarded its treatment of Yemeni workers as the utmost sacrifice, many in Yemen have viewed it as nothing but an opportunistic attempt to obtain cheap Yemeni manpower to work in professions which Saudi citizens despise. While the ordinary Saudi has viewed the many Yemeni workers in Saudi Arabia as competing with him for his legitimate livelihood, some in Yemen have believed that the kingdom has been exploiting Yemeni manpower!

The fifth complication in Yemeni–Saudi relations concerns patterns of behaviour which are spontaneous, but which unintentionally create horrible insults. Many ordinary people in the kingdom call the Yemenis 'Zaidis' (adherents of the Zaidiyah sect). Some of them try to be witty by calling the Yemeni citizen 'Abu-Yemen'. They are then completely taken aback

---

[1] Each time the Yemeni president visits the kingdom, a stupid joke circulates to the effect that the president, immediately upon entering the government guest palace rushes to repair pipes in need of a plumber!

when they visit Sanaa and hear 'hey Saudi, hey Jew'! I have tried to explain to a number of ordinary Saudi citizens that the use of a sectarian name to refer to a nationality is unjustified and a form of disparagement for the other party. I explained that this was the same psychological process that made the Saudis dislike being described as 'wahhabis'. However, my attempt apparently failed, as they saw nothing in the use of the term 'Zaidi' that would call for an angry response!

The Iraqi president succeeded in exploiting Yemeni–Gulf sensitivities in an unprecedented way. On the one hand, he appeared as the 'guarantor of Yemeni unification', which he advocated and patronised by guaranteeing to each Yemeni party the other party's adherence to its commitments. On the other hand, Saddam Hussein exploited the Yemenis' feelings of isolation *vis-à-vis* the club of the Gulf rich (the Gulf Co-operation Council). He welcomed Yemen as a founder member in the club of the Arab poor (the Arab Co-operation Council). Also, the Ba'ath Party was active in Yemen, which sometimes resulted in peculiar anomalies. For example, several tribal chiefs saw nothing strange in combining their hereditary tribal positions with membership in the leadership of the Arab Ba'ath Socialist Party. Yemeni intellectuals and Gulf intellectuals maintained almost no relationships, whereas many opportunities were provided for Yemeni writers to meet with Iraqi Ba'a-thist writers – a process which caused Yemeni intellectuals to view the Iraqi Ba'athist regime in a radiant progressive light.

It is easy to understand the positions of the other countries that aligned themselves with the Iraqi president. In Sudan, there was a ruling coalition comprising a group of officers and the fundamentalist movement of Dr Hasan al-Turabi. The face of the regime was military, and its attitudes were those of Turabi. Saddam Hussein won over the officers with enormous quantities of weapons, which he provided at no cost at a critical time when Sudan could not afford to buy the weapons these officers felt they needed to confront the rebellion in southern Sudan and to maintain Sudan's unity. As for Dr al-Turabi, he had his own calculations, discussed at length in the next chapter, which required that he support the Iraqi president.

In Algeria, the government felt no sympathy with Saddam Hussein. However, it found it in its interest to express reservations towards the decision of the Arab summit, which welcomed foreign forces. The Algerian government attempted to prevent itself from being overtaken by the fundamentalist movement, under the leadership of Dr Abbas Madani (the head of the Islamic Salvation Front) which clearly inclined toward Iraq and rallied the Algerian public to support it. If we add to this a number of intellectuals' sympathy with what they considered the 'progressive' party in the conflict, and the reflection of this sympathy in the media, the general features of Algeria's position became clear.

In Tunisia, similar considerations applied. The need to keep ahead of the fundamentalist movement compelled the Tunisian government to tilt toward Iraq. Moreover, the Tunisian President, Zine El Abidine Ben Ali, felt personal bitterness over the position of Egypt (and the Gulf countries) regarding the return of the Arab League to Cairo. Tunisia had opened its arms to the League during the period when Egypt's membership was frozen. The Tunisian president did not understand why it was now desired to transfer the League with such haste without justification and without deference to the feelings of the Tunisian people. When the Egyptian president called for an emergency summit in Cairo, the Tunisian president recommended that it be delayed for a short while to permit him to study the situation further. His recommendation was disregarded and the summit was held in his absence. All of these factors compelled the Tunisian president to believe that there was a plan to limit Tunisia's role. He felt he should prove his freedom of action.

In Mauritania, Iraqi arms once again played a significant role in creating a climate of sympathy for the Iraqi president. However, Mauritania sought to remain outside the conflict. The government was satisfied with a cautious approach. It sent letters to the Gulf countries emphasizing its respect for the right of every state to take measures which it deems appropriate to maintain its integrity. The Mauritanian position did not cause the same angry reaction in the Gulf as that of other countries.

In any case, the alliance between Iraq and these countries was really a political, media alliance. It had no significant military aspects, despite the talk of millions of volunteers who would rush in from everywhere to save Iraq. Despite the noisy demonstrations criticizing Iraq's enemies, and despite the 'popular committees' to aid Iraq, no country which sympathized with Saddam Hussein provided any appreciable military support. The 'millions' of volunteers evaporated and became a few hundred whose presence was only symbolic. Yasir 'Arafat did not fulfill his repeated promise to remain in Saddam Hussein's trench until the end. Perhaps the Iraqi president, in the depths of his heart, was as indignant over the limited support which he received from his friends as his enemies were over the fact of this support, which they imagined would be unlimited.

In this period, the anti-Iraq coalition, under the leadership of the United States, was growing daily, armed with the newest weapons and the latest resolutions of the United Nations. There was no appreciable disagreement among the industrialized countries regarding the need to thwart the Iraqi invasion, although numerous differences of opinion existed regarding the details of how it should be done. British Prime Minister Margaret Thatcher was most enthusiastic about a military operation against Iraq. This enthusiasm is attributed to Britain's historical relationship with Kuwait, and to the deep mutual enmity between her and the Iraqi president. It can also be attributed to the unbending nature of the 'Iron Lady's' personality. Many believed that the coincidence of her presence in the United States when the invasion began reinforced the American president's determination to oppose the invasion. From the outset, France opposed the Iraqi adventure. However, during the crisis, it strove to maintain for itself a freedom of manoeuvre, which was ultimately of no use because of the Iraqi president's recalcitrance. Germany and Japan, because of their constitutions, were unable to send military forces. Their contributions therefore had to be financial.

The entire industrialized world was determined to end Saddam Hussein's direct control over Kuwait's oil and his indirect control over Gulf oil. No one deviated from this consensus. Demonstrators in American and European cities criticized the principle, i.e., war! They did not defend Saddam Hussein. Even these demonstrations disappeared when Saddam Hussein polluted the Gulf. The image of a sea-bird mired in a black oil slick appeared repeatedly on television screens everywhere in the Western world. History will remember, with a mixture of irony and pain, that one sea-bird succeeded in causing an outpouring of emotion among ordinary people in the West which was more than was caused by the loss of Kuwait (or the loss of Palestine!).

The international coalition against Saddam Hussein would not have assumed a truly international character had it been limited to the Gulf states and the countries of the industrialized world. Its base had to be expanded to include Arab countries, Islamic countries, and Third World countries. In this regard, Egypt indisputably played a leading role. The Iraqi leader made a major mistake when he imagined that the Egyptian president would support the invasion of Kuwait, or at least remain neutral. Close to a million Egyptians were working in Iraq, and Saddam Hussein trusted that the Egyptian president would take this into account before making any decision. Also, the last years of the Iraqi–Iranian war had witnessed a notice-able increase in co-operation between Egypt and Iraq in differ-ent political, economic and military fields. When Egypt joined the Arab Co-operation Council, its status changed from that of a friend to an ally of Iraq. Shortly before the invasion, Saddam Hussein gave the Egyptian people a gift of $50 million, accompanied by a promise of more, as stated publicly by the Egyptian president, as a final move to pull Egypt into the Iraqi orbit.

However, all of these factors were in fact a double-edged sword. Many Egyptians complained of the treatment which they received in Iraq, especially the financial restrictions that prohibited them from transferring even a small portion of their salaries to Egypt. The unsettled accounts of Egyptians workers accumulated, until they became a thorn in the side of Iraqi–Egyptian relations. After the end of the war, a large number of Iraqi soldiers were discharged only to find that their civilian jobs had been taken over by Egyptians. It seems that this drove some of them to acts of violence against Egyptians residing in Iraq. This may be the reason why dozens of bodies arrived in Egypt from Iraq without any acceptable explanation. These incidents caused intense revulsion among many Egyptians. Also, the attempts made by the Iraqi president to contain Egypt seemed, in the Egyptian president's view, crude and primitive. In addition to all of these considerations, there were strategic calculations connected with Egyptian–American relations and Egyptian–Gulf relations. The sacrificing of all that to satisfy Saddam Hussein was not a serious option.

A constantly repeated mistake in Saddam Hussein's calculations is his assumption that the other players will behave according to their narrow interests alone, without taking any principle into account. The fact of the matter is that it is rare, if not impossible, to find a decision-maker whose decisions do not take principles into account. The Egyptian president no doubt viewed the Iraqi invasion of Kuwait, especially after the promises made by the Iraqi president, as a disgraceful act from a moral standpoint, regardless of any other consideration. When Husni Mubarak stated, throughout the entire crisis, that Egypt made its decision for reasons of principle, he was sincere. When Egypt joined the anti-Saddam Hussein coalition, this coalition gained the most populous and influential Arab country. In addition, the effectiveness of Egypt's role was enhanced by the arrival of a large number of Egyptian forces to participate in the battle.

Syria is second in importance after Egypt. With Syria's entry into the coalition, it became clear that the battle would not be between 'progressives' and 'reactionaries', as Saddam Hussein tried to depict it. If some could explain the Egyptian decision as merely a reflection of the Egyptian links with American strategy, the Syrian decision is undoubtedly impossible to explain in this way. The 'revolutionary', 'socialist' and 'nationalistic' credentials of the Syrian regime are no less than, if not superior to, those of the Iraqi regime. Syria has no doubt played a much greater role than Iraq in the Arab–Israeli conflict and has borne the burden of this conflict to a much greater degree. Some maintain that the mutual personal hatred between the Iraqi president and the Syrian president was the most important factor in Syria's decision. Others believe that the decision allowed Syria to emerge from its regional and international isolation (and gain extensive freedom to operate in Lebanon). Still others maintain that the desire to establish closer economic relations with the Gulf was the true motive. Perhaps Syria's decision was ultimately the outcome of all these considerations. Syria's joining of the coalition was a severe setback for the Iraqi plan. With Syria's entry, the coalition came to encompass countries which were clearly both on the right and left.

61

The active role played by Turkey in the coalition did not enter into Iraqi calculations. Relations between the two neighbours – despite a calm exterior, trade activity, and an oil pipeline of strategic importance to Iraq and financial importance to Turkey – were sullied by a great deal of mutual mistrust for historical and ideological reasons. Following the invasion, when Iraqi envoy Taha Yasin Ramadan tried to explain Iraq's 'historical rights' to Kuwait to the Turkish president, the latter responded immediately that he could name Iraqi areas to which Turkey has 'historical rights'. The Turkish president, Turgut Ozal, when he came to power, initiated a liberal economic policy based on linking the Turkish economy to the West. He was not about to sacrifice what he considered Turkey's future to satisfy Saddam Hussein.

Nor did the Iraqi president have better luck with Iran. Since the end of the war, negotiations between the two countries had encountered difficulties: Iran insisted on the restoration of joint sovereignty over the Shatt al-Arab waterway and Iraq's acceptance of the principle of compensation for Iran's war losses. Saddam Hussein rejected these demands, because to do otherwise would mean that his claim of victory in the war would be meaningless. The Iraqi president decided that the Kuwaiti adventure would allow him to kill two birds with one stone. He would agree to Iran's demands, so that his concession would be overlooked in the uproar over the invasion of Kuwait; in exchange, he would obtain Iran's friendship, so that it would support the adventure or at least be neutral. However, the stone hit neither bird. The concession was not concealed by the events. On the contrary, it became a strong media card in counter-propaganda. Also, the concession failed to neutralize Iran. The Iraqi president was no doubt over optimistic when he assumed that conceding what Iran considered its right would erase the legacy of a bitter war and transform Iran overnight from the scourge of the age into a tender, loving friend. He also failed miserably, for example, to understand the ruling ayatollahs in Teheran when he imagined that he could attract them to his side in the battle of 'belief versus disbelief' by promoting Islamic slogans. Throughout the crisis, Iran maintained a practical, logical position dictated by its interests. It generously granted Iraq's wish to end the war officially and normalize relations; it condemned the invasion of

Kuwait strongly and refused to recognize any regional changes resulting from it; and it contented itself with verbally criticizing the foreign presence. Iran emerged from the crisis with normal relations with Iraq, friendly relations with the Gulf, and better relations with the industrialized world.

In one camp was Saddam Hussein, a group of small states, and noisy demonstrations in the streets. On the other side was what Saddam Hussein called the 'abominable coalition': 33 countries representing the aggregate financial, technological, political and military weight of the entire world. The result did not require astrologers to predict. Although, in the minds of people throughout the Arab world, a leaflet was circulated in Arab capitals containing a prophecy from an ancient book, which claimed that a man named 'Sadim' would defeat the world, and that they would 'witness the miracle between the months of Jumada [the sixth month of the Muslim year] and Rajab [the seventh month of the Muslim year]'!

4

THE PROPAGANDA BATTLE

Some defend the state with swords
Some with drums.

al-Mutanabbi

According to the Iraqi media story, there had been a domestic uprising against the ruling regime in Kuwait; the revolution asked for the assistance of Iraq, which was compelled by its national duty to respond to the 'call' of the new revolutionary government. (To corroborate this myth, the city of al-Ahmadi was renamed the 'City of the Call', and the Iraqi newspaper which began to be published in Kuwait was entitled *The Call*.) This was the only justification that appeared in the Iraqi media during the initial days of the invasion. The Iraqi media were bent on not inciting any Gulf country. It aimed its entire attack on the amir of Kuwait, whom it referred to as 'Croesus'.[1] Saddam Hussein wanted to assure the Gulf countries that Kuwait was a 'special case' that would not be repeated.

After a few days, it became clear that no one believed the fable of the 'domestic revolution' or the myth of the 'provisional revolutionary government'. A new media cover was needed. This time, it was 'the return of the branch to the root'. Legitimate intervention turned into immediate unification through merger, and the Iraqi media changed from talking about an imminent withdrawal to 'the happiness of citizens everywhere with this eternal, historical achievement of unification'. When it became clear that the Gulf countries did not recognize the new situation, the Gulf leaders became 'bedouins', the Kingdom of Saudi Arabia became the 'lands of Najd and al-Hijaz', and two radio broadcasts were designated to attack these 'lands' – 'Radio Mecca' and 'Radio Medina'. As Arab opposition to the invasion emerged, the scope of the

[1] Throughout the crisis, numerous press reports emphasized that the Iraqi president's personal wealth far exceeded that of the amir of Kuwait!

69

attack was expanded, and 'Radio Egypt of Arabism' was resurrected from its grave. When the opposition of the industrial countries emerged, the Iraqi media became more ambitious. The operation to occupy Kuwait became 'the great clash' between faith and unbelief. Shortly thereafter, this clash developed into the 'mother of battles' of all history. Baghdad's official radio broadcast was designated 'Radio Mother of Battles'.

It is strange that the Iraqi president, following the war, dismissed his culture and information minister from his post. Fairness would have required the minister to remain in his position, since it was ultimately only on the media front that Iraq fought with some measure of competence and effectiveness. This distinguished this front from the diplomatic front, which was embroiled daily in contradictory initiatives, and the military front, which collapsed like sand castles.

The Iraqi media strategy was simplicity itself: to appeal to every taste. The Iraqi media came to resemble a large auction, offering the public all the goods which it sought. Thus the slogan 'linkage' was intended to satisfy the Palestinians. God's believing servant (Saddam Hussein) offered his Islamic slogans to attract all believers. The slogan of 'unity' aimed to satisfy nationalists. Finally, the slogan 'distribution of the wealth' was designed to attract the enthusiasm of all the Arab poor.

The Iraqi media became a theatre of the absurd. The actors would deviate from the text, come down off the stage, and move among the ranks of the spectators, making up for each row a play especially tailored to it. Stranger still, the viewers clapped and demanded more. In the Iraqi media, Saddam Hussein became a wondrous study in contrasts: the heretical secularist who now declared that he was a holy warrior of Islam; the hero of al-Qadisiyah[1] who has now become a friend of Iran; the wealthy distributor of the wealth; and the man of the people who belongs to the noblest Arab family.

The confrontation surrounding Kuwait indeed became the 'mother of battles'. Anyone who had a quarrel with Israel, with the ruling regime in his country, with Western civilization, or opposed the stagnation of the Arab world entered the battle. Thus, the Palestinian who dreams of a return to Jaffa lined

[1]The name of the battle where Arab Muslim armies defeated the Persian Zoroastrian empire in the early years of Islam.

up behind Saddam Hussein, as did the Moroccan who feels degraded as he works in the port of Marseilles, the Algerian who is still experiencing the nightmare of colonialism, and the 'fundamentalist' who wants to apply Islamic law in Sudan. The process began with the occupation of Kuwait but then Kuwait was almost forgotten as every party came with its own cause to hear from the Iraqi media something about it that would gladden its heart.

The Gulf media, like Kuwait itself, were taken by surprise. The Gulf media are peaceful and restrained. They are thus easily taken by surprise. During the past decade, the Gulf media were extremely sympathetic to Saddam Hussein. The Iraqi president's receptions were a nightly spectacle on every Gulf television network. It was not easy for the Gulf media to go on to the offensive. Nor was it an easy matter to deal with a dear friend who, in the space of hours, had become a dangerous enemy. The Gulf media were initially struck by total paralysis. As we stated above, all the broadcasts of the world were reporting the details of the invasion minute by minute, except for the broadcasts of the countries being threatened by an invasion (Gulf newspapers reported the facts as conveyed to them by news agencies without commentary!).

Gradually, as the Gulf governments recovered from the shock, the Gulf media began to regain their balance. Their first scoop was the broadcast of interviews with Kuwaitis fleeing from the Iraqi occupation. Those interviews – with their spontaneity, authenticity, scenes of tears being shed, homeless children, the old woman who challenged Saddam Hussein to meet her face to face – were a slap in the face of Iraqi claims. The broadcast of these interviews created a warm wave of sympathy towards Kuwait and a raging wave of anger against the Iraqi president (the extent of this wave cannot be imagined by anyone who was not then in the Gulf). At the time, an Algerian friend told me that had these interviews been broadcast by the Algerian media, they would have reversed Algerian public opinion. The Gulf media were undoubtedly remiss in not conveying these interviews to the largest possible number of viewers throughout the entire world. If millions had been spent to hire the largest public relations firms, no more effective programmes could have been produced. Although the exodus of large numbers of Kuwaitis led to the development of some sensitivity between the 'emigrés' and those who remained in Kuwait to mount resistance, it also led, from a purely media standpoint, to the collapse of the myth of the 'return of the branch to the root'. The 'branch', as seen by the entire world, preferred being hurled into the unknown to being attached to the 'root'!

The Gulf media shifted to the attack. The attack was violent and sharp. It assumed a form unknown in the history of the Gulf media, which were previously accustomed to referring to a head of state as 'his excellency' even when relations were most critical. The Gulf media responded to insult with insult. Perhaps the media were the first to be surprised by the combativeness slumbering deep within them, and which awoke in response to the calamity. For the first time, something more than the presentation of tranquil media reports was being produced.

In addition, stirring songs rang out everywhere, splendid in form and content. The Gulf was pervaded by a nationalistic spirit known only by countries at war. The media faithfully conveyed that spirit. Gulf citizens had never entered a war of any kind in modern times. The scenes of young volunteers and the destruction in Kuwait as well as nationalistic speeches struck a sensitive chord within Gulf citizens. A Gulf official asked, seriously but with a smile: 'Is there hope of the spirit of the war continuing after the war?'

None the less, the Gulf media's success did not transcend the Gulf. In the Arab world, the Egyptian media battled with the Iraqi media. The Egyptian president himself was the star of the Egyptian media. Not one day passed without a press conference, speech, or open message directed at the Iraqi president. The secrets broadcast by President Husni Mubarak regarding the Arab Co-operation Council and Saddam Hussein's attempts to attract Egypt into his orbit constituted rich, provocative media material.

The Gulf media could have acted more effectively. However, they concentrated all their efforts and abilities on the domestic scene. The well known Kuwaiti preacher Shaykh Ahmad al-Qattan, was able in one sermon, to turn out tens of thousands of Algerians to demonstrate against Saddam Hussein. But there was only one such sermon. The Gulf media failed to reach the masses in the wider Islamic world. The effect of this

72

failure was clear in countries such as Pakistan, India, Indonesia and Malaysia. Among the surprises of the crisis was the support given by many Islamic groups in these countries to the Iraqi president, despite the strong, numerous ties that bound these countries with the Gulf states. In the later stages of the crisis, the Gulf countries began to reach for the Islamic world and that yielded immediate results. However, everything undertaken in this regard was too late and of limited effect.

However, the success achieved by the Iraqi media in the Arab arena was not so much based on the superiority of its technology or personnel as on the desire of the masses to hear what it was saying. As this desire grew, the effectiveness of this media increased. In Western countries, where the Iraqi media's slogans mean nothing, the Iraqi media's effectiveness was limited and perhaps exercised a negative influence. This ranged from the Iraqi president, who would regale the Western public with boring, condescending explanations and digressions, as if he were speaking to backward elementary school pupils, to his ambassadors who would speak in London, Washington and Paris as if they were broadcasters of the Voice of the Masses in Baghdad. The Iraqi media in the West were unquestionably a disaster.[1] It suffices here to refer to what happened when a mutual understanding was reached whereby the American president was to address the Iraqi people in a video to be broadcast by the Iraqi media and the Iraqi president was to address American people in a video to be broadcast by the American media. The American president spoke succinctly for no more than ten minutes, whereas the Iraqi president spoke boringly for more than an hour. I doubt whether anyone in the United States, other than specialists, listened to him from beginning to end. By contrast, Gulf officials were able to address the Western public fairly effectively due to their better understanding of the Western

---

[1] In Amman, a British journalist asked Taha Yasin Ramadan (the first deputy prime minister) why foreign journalists were being prevented from visiting Kuwait. He responded that it was a military zone, and that 'he would break the leg' of any journalist who went there. In Baghdad, the minister of culture and information stated to an American television network that the Iraqi people 'would eat' captured American paratroopers. In Washington, the Iraqi ambassador to the United Nations sent an American who spoke to him reeling, because she called him by his first name instead of 'his excellency the ambassador'. We can imagine the effect of all this on the Western public.

mentality and the fact that they were defending a cause that enjoyed the sympathy of listeners. The truth is that the greatest, most eloquent, and most persuasive advocate could not have defended the occupation of Kuwait convincingly in the vast sea of hostile sentiment toward Saddam Hussein in the West. Even politicians known for their extensive experience in dealing with the Western media, such as King Hussein and his heir apparent, Prince Hasan, lost all credibility in the West by merely appearing to align themselves with Saddam Hussein.

Here, we must acknowledge with shame that both the Gulf and the Iraqi media descended to a frightening level of abuse. No one hesitated before mounting an attack of any sort. The prevalent belief was that, in battles of life and death, it is permitted to use all weapons (it must not be forgotten that the danger of Iraqi gases was always present during the confrontation). Also, neither of the two sides refrained from 'improving' facts or inventing them altogether. A person listening to radio broadcasts coming out of Baghdad would imagine that the entire Saudi people was demonstrating against its government and that dozens of demonstrators were being killed daily, whereas a person reading Gulf newspapers would discover, daily, a conspiracy in Baghdad, whose victims were usually 'Izzat Ibrahim and 'Oddi, Saddam Hussein's eldest son. I questioned the utility of all of these lies and doubted their effectiveness until I met a press delegation from a North African country, whose members told me that they were 'surprised' when they visited the Holy Mosque in Mecca and the Prophet's Mosque without finding American forces 'besieging' them. Some even believed the fable aired by Radio Baghdad about the pig (the consumption of which is forbidden by Islam) units brought by American soldiers. This generated a Saudi joke to the effect that the bringing of the pigs became possible only because they were declared at customs as 'sheep wearing gas masks'. However, it is certain that some of the Iraqi exaggerations damaged Iraq's cause. Radio Baghdad spoke daily of violent struggles among the different forces in the coalition and of the fatal diseases from which no American soldier is safe. It also spoke of the destructive effect of the desert environment on equipment and personnel. There is no doubt that the daily repetition of these reports did nothing to bolster the morale of Iraqi soldiers.

During this period, the Arab media was split along lines that paralleled the political split. The countries that supported the Iraqi president politically supported him in the media, and the countries that opposed him politically attacked him in the media. The media in the countries which remained neutral were neutral. A writer rarely adopted a position that differed from that of his government. A newspaper rarely advocated a policy that contradicted governmental policy (almost all exceptions came from Egypt; a tribute to its relative freedom). 'Popular' initiatives were nothing but governmental or quasi-governmental measures, whether they were 'popular' volunteer centres or 'popular' committees to aid Iraq. Thus, it once again became clear that the Arab media are born from the state, grow and develop under its protection, and die and are buried by the state.

However, the crisis brought to the fore, especially in the Gulf, a new form of the media which we can call the 'unconventional media' or 'counter-media' and which transcend the customary media – radio, television and newspapers. These media sometimes assume the form of pamphlets made possible by the technological revolution; they are printed on computers instead of being written by hand and are sent via fax instead of being distributed in the streets. At other times, the counter-media assume the form of cassette tapes which enjoy a brisk circulation. Throughout the Arab world, the Friday sermon (on cassette) has spread on an unprecedented scale.

The task of monitoring the counter-media is much more difficult than monitoring the official media and is still awaiting researchers. None the less, it can be said that the counter-media in the Gulf agreed with the official media in arousing sympathy for the Kuwaiti people. However, it differed with them over how to handle the crisis. It advocated 'Islamic Jihad' instead of seeking the assistance of foreign forces, which indicates that the counter-media were governed by 'fundamentalist' attitudes at least in some aspects.

The Western media entered the confrontation in their typical fashion. These media agreed with their governments on strategy but disagreed with them on details. When the crisis being faced by a Western country concerns a primary national

interest, the media, despite all their outward and real independence, become merely a national policy tool. However, if the
Arab media follow their governments because they are forced
to do so, the Western media follow their governments wil-
lingly. In the West, the same factors that produce a political
decision produce a media decision. Public opinion polls are an
example. The effect of these polls on members of the media
is no less than their effect on political leaders. The same applies
to party, trade union, religious and social pressures. At the
same time, the area of disagreement between the government
and the media is large in matters of detail. This disagreement
is what makes the Western media interesting and exciting,
unlike the parrot-like Arab media.

The Western media generally opposed the invasion of
Kuwait and the continuation of Iraq's occupation of Kuwait.
This position corresponded with governmental policies. Apart
from this fundamental principle, there were numerous viewpoints in the Western media which differed considerably from
official viewpoints, and which were disseminated freely. Thus,
we heard commentator after commentator criticize the military
option and call for continuing the economic blockade. We also
saw conference after conference warn of the consequences of
war and the large number of expected casualties. The Western
media continued to convey Iraqi viewpoints, completely
untroubled by the accusations of 'disloyalty' levelled against
them by some viewers.

There were a few voices in the Western media that appeared
to be accepting the *fait accompli* presented by the invasion and
reaching a mutual understanding with Saddam Hussein. Chief
among them were Edward Heath, a former British prime minister, and Ramsey Clark, a former US attorney general. However, such views were the exception that proved the rule.
Their dissemination proved the Western media's independence
without affecting its actual orientation.

This two-fold nature of the Western media – agreement with
the governments on principle and disagreement with them
regarding the details – confused many in the Arab world and
left doubts about the Western media's credibility. Supporters
of the Iraqi president noted that the attitudes of the Western
media did not differ from the attitudes of the Western governments. Therefore, they lost confidence in them, even when

they reported events faithfully. Perhaps this explains why many refused to believe Iraq's military defeat, even when they saw it with their own eyes on television. At the same time, many of the Iraqi president's adversaries, in the Gulf especially, were surprised by the Western media's extensive coverage of activities sympathetic to Saddam Hussein, whether a demonstration in Tunisia, a conference in Amman, or a statement by an Arab association in the United States. Those who were confused were unable to understand this phenomenon. Sometimes they attributed it to Iraqi bribery. At other times they attributed it to Palestinian penetration of the BBC! The Iraqi president's supporters failed to see that the strategic alignment of the Western media with their governments did not prevent them from reporting on actual events with considerable objectivity. Saddam Hussein's enemies failed to see that partiality of the Western media in favour of Iraq where it occurred was no more than a footnote on a large page filled with strident attacks against the Iraqi president.

During the gulf crisis, CNN's star rose, not only in the West, but everywhere, proving the old adage that 'one people's misfortunes are another's fortunes'. This television channel, which was established in 1980, has been a revolutionary concept in the media world. It specializes in news and political commentary without the customary entertainment programmes which no one could imagine a television station dispensing with for a single day. Contrary to all expectations, the station has succeeded. It enjoys widespread diffusion, and it has proved its economic feasibility. During the crisis, this channel became the main source of news everywhere it was received. We heard president after president and official after official explaining that he obtained his information from this channel. It is enough to say here that the reports which the station transmitted from Baghdad were the first indication of the success of the initial air strike.

During the crisis, CNN was received in Gulf homes in most cases for the first time. The decision by the relevant information ministers to allow its direct broadcast was a courageous one from more than one standpoint. The decision was made despite a storm of criticism, and it led to an unflattering comparison between the Western media and the Arab (and Gulf) media. If we can excuse those who find something disagreeable in the channel's programmes (manifestations of clear support for Israel received the most criticism), we should remind opponents of CNN that what they do not like will not simply cease to exist through their merely not viewing it on television. This channel is an omen of things to come. The Arabs can no longer refuse to enter the satellite age. Nor can they fight missiles with daggers, knowledge with sorcery, and nuclear weapons with talismans. The entire world has become a 'single electronic village'. This does not have to be licensed by any information ministry. The Arabs have a clear choice: to deal with the fact with courage and enthusiasm or with cowardice and hesitancy.

Short-wave radio unleashed an enormous revolution in communications. It enabled our fathers to listen to Hitler's speeches as he was delivering them. Satellites unleashed an even more powerful revolution that is enabling us to watch Yeltsin as he speaks. Only God knows what our children and their children will be able to see and hear (and perhaps smell!). With the advent of short-wave radio, the task of controlling thought became difficult (despite jamming devices). With the advent of satellites, this task has become almost impossible (despite the development of jamming methods). In the future, the censor will inevitably become extinct as the dinosaur. The extinction of the censor has implications that are graver than those which accompanied the extinction of dinosaur. The most important is that no one will be able to repel a cultural invasion by seizing publications and adding to the lists of forbidden items. Years from now, a normal television set will be able to pick up any programme transmitted by satellite. This is a daily reality in the life of the Western citizen, who can switch between dozens of stations in different parts of the world. Within a short time, it will also be a daily reality in the life of the Arab citizen.

Naturally, comparisons began to be made between the Western media and the Arab media. The result has been painful. Hundreds of Western correspondents have spent many years covering wars and reporting news from every capital. By contrast, Arab 'correspondents' have had to be satisfied with consuming what the news agencies transmit to them. During the crisis, enormous armies of Western experts in every field, from politics to spying to poison gases, appeared in the media.

By contrast, Arab experts were limited to a small number of diplomats, and military people who spoke with a great deal of reservation. The Arab viewer discovered the enormous difference between the Western programme host – his understanding of the topic of discussion, freedom to ask questions, and constant disagreement with guests on the programme – and the Arab programme host, who, with great timidity, inquires as to the opinion of 'his excellency' the guest, and nods his head in admiration and confirmation even before his excellency the guest begins to talk.

We can say that the Iraqi media ultimately proved their superiority over the competing media in the Arab arena, which is the main battlefield. However, this superiority did not prevent the defeat of Iraq. The Arab media succeeded in exploiting Arab differences, but could not transform them into political power with influence over the course of events. It is likely that the Iraqi president believed the ordinary Arab's sympathy with him to be much greater than it actually was. Saddam Hussein repeatedly said to a number of his visitors that the coalition would not dare attack Iraq but that, if an attack took place, every Arab government participating in the coalition would be toppled. (He was depending on the ordinary Arab to achieve this outcome). When Desert Storm broke out, Arab streets did not catch fire. On the contrary, the people stood quietly and dumbfounded, watching what was happening with noticeable calm.

The media 'mother of battles' did not teach us a single new lesson. However, it did underscore the soundness of three old lessons. The first is that the media are a primary element of national policy in times of peace and war, domestically and abroad. The second is that the media, as long as they are not equipped with up-to-date technology and do not embrace the age of satellites, will continue to be limited in their effectiveness and influence. The third is that the media, regardless of their capabilities and achievements, cannot dispense with the political, economic and military base on which they rest, and with which they ultimately rise or fall.

5

THE HEIRS' EXPECTATIONS

He who departs
Is plundered by him who succeeds.

al-Mutanabbi

I have used the expression 'fundamentalists' in these pages knowing that it is the literal Arabic translation of a term that originated in the West to describe mostly protestant Christian groups. My usage conforms with that which is prevalent both in the Arabic press and in everyday usage. I have placed quotation marks around the word to indicate that I am using it in a technical sense. The time has come to clarify what I mean by the term.

In these pages, the word 'fundamentalists' applies only to parties that seek power and promote Islamic slogans. This definition clarifies the great difference between the fundamentalist phenomenon and a number of phenomena in the Arab, Islamic arena which are sometimes mistaken for 'fundamentalist' in a way which leads to chaotic and confused judgements.

'Fundamentalism' in the sense that it is used here has no connection with the 'Islamic awakening' which means a rediscovery by Muslims of themselves, their creed, identity, and cultural distinction. This Islamic awakening expresses itself in numerous social, cultural, spiritual, and behavioural spheres. Limiting the definition of the Islamic awakening to the phenomenon of political parties does not do justice to the truth. At present, I am not so much concerned with debating the nature of the relation between 'fundamentalism' and the Islamic awakening, or whether fundamentalism is a negative or a positive aspect of the Islamic awakening, as I am with emphasizing that I do not consider the two terms synonymous. Nor do I regard the two phenomena as two sides of the same coin.

'Fundamentalism', according to my definition, has no

relation to personal piety. A Muslim might be extremely pious and adhere to every commandment and prohibition in Islamic law, both minor and major, without being a member of a political party that aims to obtain power. Likewise, a member of a 'fundamentalist' political party is not necessarily more pious than other Muslims, and may not be religious at all[1] (it is also not necessary for a member of a socialist party to be poor!). On the other hand, despite what many think, there is no connection between 'fundamentalism' and 'puritanism' or 'fanaticism'. A Muslim might be 'puritanical' to the point of self-deprivation, or an extreme fanatic, without being a fundamentalist, and a 'fundamentalist' does not necessarily have to be puritanical or fanatic.

The discussion of 'political parties' excludes from the sphere of 'fundamentalism' Islamic groups that carry out missionary work without assuming the form of a party or organization. Also excluded are Islamic organizations whose activity is limited to social, welfare, reform or educational goals. When I speak of 'Islamic slogans', I aim to distinguish between 'fundamentalist' parties and parties that promote slogans of another type, whether nationalist, Marxist or secularist. I am neutral on the question of whether or not the 'fundamentalist' parties are serious about the implementation of their slogans. My only objective is to describe, not to praise or blame.

For the sake of accuracy, I should stress that the entire discussion is virtually limited to the leadership of the 'fundamentalist' parties, and excludes the masses affiliated with them. The organization of these parties is an exact replica of communist party organization, with a minor change in designations, so that the 'cell' becomes the 'community', the central committee becomes the 'consultative committee', and the 'general secretary' becomes the 'supreme guide'. In this type of organization, power is concentrated at the apex of a pyramid, despite any references to 'consultation'. The role of the base is limited virtually to the implementation of orders coming

---

[1] A Saudi conservative scholar believes that Arab 'fundamentalists', if they were truly pious, would be concerned with 'removing graven images from the mosques, apostasy from the heart, and innovation from religious observances, and they would not restrict their activity to promoting slogans that satisfy the demagogic majority of voters.'

from above, with enthusiasm driven by party discipline as much as by religious sentiment.

The masses affiliated with these parties contain a broad sector of idealists who are driven to join the movement only by the highest and noblest motives. Only shallow observers believe that every person who joins a 'fundamentalist' movement is motivated by selfish considerations. Those who explain the phenomenon of 'fundamentalism' in purely economic terms ignore the fact that a number of 'fundamentalists' cannot be considered poor by any objective criterion. Or they ignore the fact that many of them give more to the movement than they take out. Social and political necessity are not the keys to the psyches of this sector. Many 'fundamentalists' proceed from a profound commitment to a creed that transcends their selves and direct interests. They are searching for a more beautiful tomorrow, in which the values of justice, purity and chastity are widespread. A pious, God-fearing youth, who abstains from pleasures, looks down upon passions, and adheres to Islam inwardly and outwardly as he understands it, does not do so to become a leader or obtain a position. He does so out of a profound, internal conviction.

In addition to this idealistic sector among the masses of 'fundamentalism' there is a broad sector of the 'humiliated' or 'crushed' (or 'the oppressed', to use a Quranic term whose use has been popularized by the Islamic revolution in Iran). In this case, the motive for joining a 'fundamentalist' organization is a powerful human desire to eliminate political and social injustice. Who can blame an unemployed person if he supports a party that promises him a job? Who can blame a homeless person if he follows a leader who promises him housing?

However, it is not my concern here to digress into an analysis of 'fundamentalism'. I am compelled to discuss it only because of the substantial role played by 'fundamentalist' leaders during the crisis. These leaders were responsible for attracting large sectors of public opinion to the Iraqi president's camp. This position was the exact opposite of the position that would be expected in the light of the history of the 'fundamentalist' movement and past precedents. Like the Palestinian position, the 'fundamentalist' position came as a total surprise.

According to all indications, the 'fundamentalist' movement

should have opposed Saddam Hussein's Kuwaiti adventure, or at least taken a neutral stand on it, purely for doctrinal reasons. Never since Kamal Ataturk has there been a leader in the Islamic world who is as clearly and decisively secular as the Iraqi leader. Saddam Hussein believes, in his words, that 'the modern Arab state must avoid becoming a house of worship or a deliverer of formal legal opinions for a religious way of life'[1] at the same time as the 'fundamentalist' programme was basing itself on the need for the state to be the deliverer of formal legal opinions for a religious way of life. Saddam Hussein adds that basing the ordinances of government on religion necessarily 'hinders development in the affairs of life and transforms life into an unbearable hell', because doing so would 'empty religion of its sacredness, awe and spirit.'[2] In other words, the Iraqi president believes that the application of Islamic law is an affront to both religion and the temporal world. Saddam Hussein adds that all matters must be discussed in a scientific way which 'excludes from the discussion all things spiritual.'[3] This is to say that Islam has no connection whatsoever to any decision. The religion with which Saddam Hussein can coexist does not go beyond permitting all people to 'practice their regular religious rituals', provided that these rituals do not conflict with the state's policy. Otherwise, such people will be subject to severe punishment and the iron fist of the revolution.[4] The Iraqi president was not satisfied with the deletion of the state from the equation 'Islam is a religion and a state'. Rather, he established conditions for the practice of religion. Even the age of ignorance (pre-Islamic times) acquired a splendid cultural sheen in the Iraqi leader's view, because it would be unreasonable for God to choose for his mission 'the most decadent nation on earth'.[5] This was at a time when we also see the 'fundamentalists' categorizing those phenomena of life not to their liking as the 'modern age of ignorance'. In Saddam Hussein's view, the only advantage offered by religion is that it can be used 'as a tool of resistance and a weapon'. Even such use of religion

[1] See Amir Iskandar, *Saddam Husayn, Warrior, Thinker, and Human Being*, Paris, Hachette, 1981, p. 322.
[2] *Ibid.*, p. 322.
[3] *Ibid.*, p. 319.
[4] *Ibid.*, p. 165.
[5] *Ibid.*, p. 124.

must be carried out extremely cautiously to avoid 'revitalizing backward ideas and theories'.[1] The Iraqi leader was thus consistent with himself and his concept of religion when he 'borrowed' Islamic slogans during the Iraqi–Iranian war, and when he used them intensively during the Gulf crisis. There is no doubt that those who thought that Saddam Hussein had become an Islamic leader by merely adopting Islamic slogans were more Saddamist than Saddam Hussein himself.

Logic states that the expressesion of secularism and disdain for religion in such a well defined, glaring manner would constitute the greatest challenge to any movement that derives all its existence from religion. This was the consideration which made a segment of the 'fundamentalist' Arab movement sympathize with Iran during the Iraqi–Iranian war, despite sectarian differences (between Sunni fundamentalists in the Arab world and the Shi'ite fundamentalists in Iran). Hence, the 'fundamentalist' inclination toward Saddam Hussein during the Gulf crisis requires reflection and analysis.

The picture is further complicated by the fact that the 'fundamentalist' movement, over the years, was closely linked with the Gulf, and with Saudi Arabia in particular. The Gulf countries, whether through individuals, organizations or governments, were a primary source of funding for the 'fundamentalist' movement. The *ulema* of the kingdom were sympathetic towards the 'fundamentalist' movement. This sympathy took different forms. The government of the kingdom felt, as a matter of principle, compelled to assist any movement advocating the application of Islamic law, even if such help resulted in some political losses.[2]

More important than all this is that the occupation of Kuwait came in the form of a perfidious, surprise attack in blatant disregard of all treaties and principles. From a purely theoretical standpoint, the invasion ignored all Islamic principles that command brotherhood, co-operation, the fulfillment of promises, and deference to the right of a neighbour, and which prohibit injustice, oppression and aggression. From a purely theoretical standpoint, a secular government carried out a blat-

---

[1]*Ibid.*, p. 224.
[2]Tunisian–Saudi relations were strained, for example, by tension stemming from what the Tunisian Government considered Saudi support for the fundamentalist movement of Rached Ghannouchi.

ant act of aggression against a peaceful neighbour linked closely to the 'fundamentalist' movement. One would have assumed that the 'fundamentalist' reaction would be absolute support for the victim of the aggression. However, what actually happened did not accord with pure theory.

I have attempted in these pages, when discussing the motives that induce a decision-maker to take a particular step, to analyse matters as they appear to the decision-maker himself, not as they appear to me or other observers. We can now dispense with conjecture and guesswork, because we have a sufficient explanation of the background of the 'fundamentalist' position on the Gulf crisis. This explanation is provided by Dr Hasan al-Turabi usually a man of few words. Dr al-Turabi is a new type of 'fundamentalist' leader. His qualifications differ radically from those of the traditional leader. Al-Turabi obtained a bachelor's degree and a master's degree in law from London University. He then obtained a doctorate in comparative law from Paris. He is extremely proficient in English, French and German. It is an oddity of fate that a man so imbued with all of this 'secular' education would become the most important 'fundamentalist' leader, not only in Sudan, but throughout the Arab world.

Until the ascendancy of al-Turabi's star, the organization of the Muslim Brotherhood, with its headquarters in Cairo, was the international leader of the 'fundamentalist' movement everywhere. However, this organization proved, in the view of many 'fundamentalist' youths, unable to undertake rapid political action. It also was lacking in its understanding of the domestic conditions in each Islamic country, and this compelled the centre of gravity to shift gradually to the Islamic Political Council, which al-Turabi heads in Khartoum. Al-Turabi demonstrated a superior ability to adapt to different circumstances and emerge with advantages for the 'fundamentalist' movement. He has proved that he is more suited to lead the movement than the traditional leadership, because he is more able than it 'to achieve a balance between the transitoriness and eternal continuity of time, between the local and the universal, and between what is relative to place and time, and what is absolute in terms of eternity and existence.'

Al-Turabi considers the Gulf crisis a positive phenomenon. He believes that it is 'a landmark in the development of a new world'. The reason for this is related neither to Iraq nor Kuwait, but to the 'fundamentalist' movement: 'It is the first time that the area is witnessing the coming together of all Islamic currents with the intent to enter into events as a sincere, active participant.' The picture during the crisis differed from the old picture, in which the 'fundamentalists' 'isolated themselves from public life, contributing nothing to it or remaining satisfied with issuing communiqués from afar.' The foreign military presence, in al-Turabi's outlook, is a blessing, not punishment: 'The Americans' presence in the region only provides a means for the Islamic movement.' Moreover, al-Turabi went so far as to say: 'God has soldiers whom he mobilizes in the service of the truth. The Americans' presence on holy ground will bring together the entire Islamic movement.'

In this cold, calm view, the crisis is transformed into a 'positive landmark', because it benefited the 'fundamentalist' movement. As for the American soldiers, they became God's soldiers, because their presence served the movement (we can imagine the 'fundamentalist' position towards a 'secularist' who declares that the Americans are soldiers of God!). The goal of the movement is to put an end to 'the regimes that are ignorant of Islam as regards politics and wealth'. This remark of course includes all existing Arab regimes, but especially the Gulf regimes, which were the object of a concentrated attack by al-Turabi: 'These regimes will not continue. Any attempt to perpetuate them through the Gulf Co-operation Council will not succeed, and the failure of the current attempt to topple them does not preclude a repetition of the attempt. There will be other rounds in the future.'

Al-Turabi attacked the *ulema* who supported Kuwait during the crisis, and he expressed the belief that these *ulema* 'are not proficient at evaluating political matters. They do not study reports on political matters. They do not even read the daily newspapers.' It is notable that al-Turabi does not accuse the *ulema* of ignorance with respect to matters of jurisprudence. Rather, he accuses them of poorly evaluating 'political matters' (which are the most important in his view). Al-Turabi expresses his regret, because the 'fundamentalist' movement achieved only a limited success in the Gulf because of the *ulema*. He praises a new sector of this movement, and he hopes that it will expand its activity as the result (happy of course!) of the foreign presence and 'the clear secularization that it is causing'.

Al-Turabi sees no shame in co-operating with the Iraqi Ba'ath Party, because this party 'has now become firmly rooted in Islam and realizes that its eternal mission is the mission of Islam.' Al-Turabi provides a rationale for an alliance with any nationalist movement if such an alliance is in the interest of the 'fundamentalist' movement. However, al-Turabi criticizes the movement for its ignorance of reality, and he calls on it to 'come down from its theoretical perch' and face the facts, which are based on 'relations which concern the neighbour-hood, the nation, and the people, i.e. on nationalism.' Based on this premise, any alliance whose establishment is deemed appropriate by the 'fundamentalist' movement is not only con-sidered permissible from an Islamic outlook, it also enters 'into the context of the worship of God, the sublime and exalted'.[1]

It is clear that there is a large disparity between the tra-ditional view of the Muslim Brotherhood and this view of al-Turabi. The Muslim Brotherhood has based its positions on Islamic values, without giving the political reality the attention that it deserves. This utopian view has led to one serious setback after another for the Muslim Brotherhood, starting with the clash with the Nasirist regime in the 1950s and ending with the clash with the Syrian regime in the 1980s. In contrast to the Muslim Brotherhood, al-Turabi's movement appears flexible, dynamic and respectful of reality, even when it is trying to change it. It has been able to alter its positions quite freely while all its political decisions utlimately 'enter the path of the worship of God'.

Perhaps those who were jolted by the 'fundamentalist' leaders' position on the invasion of the Gulf would be less surprised if they realized that this position has no relation, in the view of 'fundamentalist' leaders, to Saddam Hussein, the Kuwaiti government, or the invasion itself. This position stems, from the effect of the invasion on the 'fundamentalist' movement. The 'fundamentalist' decision, like that of any pol-itical party, was based solely on the party's interest. This

[1] See the interview with Hasan al-Turabi in the *al Jami'ah* magazine, which is published by the Khartoum University Students' Union, November 1990, pp. 13–21.

interest required exploiting the crisis to topple the 'regimes that are ignorant of Islam', and Kuwait's fate became a marginal issue lacking the same importance.

Individuals who sympathize with the 'fundamentalist' movement in the Gulf were surprised by the 'fundamentalist' positions of sympathy with Saddam Hussein. Their reactions differed. Among them were those who aligned themselves with Kuwait, their national loyalty overcoming any party consideration, and there were those whose party loyalty overcame their national affiliation. In the throes of the crisis, we found some Kuwaiti citizens stating that the true problem was not with Saddam Hussein, but with the 'Jews and Christians'. Then there were those who took the middle ground, viewing the invasion of Kuwait and the foreigners' arrival to liberate it with the same severity.

Until recently, it was not accurate to speak of a fundamentalist movement in the Gulf. Kuwait was the only place in which Islamic party activity occurred and this was wholly concerned with matters of social reform. Representatives of the Gulf in the Muslim Brotherhood movement were usually naturalized persons. In Saudi Arabia, the entire people is considered 'fundamentalist', and it was contradictory to speak of a 'fundamentalist' movement in a 'fundamentalist' state (when Hasan al-Banna the founder of the Muslim Brotherhood asked King ʿAbd al-ʿAziz for permission to open a branch of the Muslim Brotherhood movement in the kingdom, the king responded that 'we are all Muslim brothers here'). However, the new 'sector' of which Dr Hasan al-Turabi speaks is not a figment of his imagination. During the crisis, a religious current did indeed break away from the religious 'establishment'.

Since the establishment of the first Saudi state close to two hundred and fifty years ago, there has been an alliance between the political leadership, represented in the Al Saʿud family, and the religious leadership, which was represented by Shaykh Muhammad Ibn ʿAbd al-Wahhab, and then the *ulema*. Over the years, this alliance has proved its solidity and strength in the face of all pressures and crises. There was an unwritten agreement, according to which the political leadership deferred to the religious leadership regarding all matters of doctrine and of direct concern to the religious leadership, such as education and the judiciary. The political leadership undertook the actual conduct of the domestic and foreign affairs of state (with the understanding that it would not violate any stipulation in the Quran or the Sunna – that is the statements and actions of the Prophet, later established as legally binding precedents in addition to the law established by the Quran). Although there were disagreements from time to time, although the religious leadership would have desired greater commitment on the part of the political leadership, and although the political leadership frequently wished for less severity on the part of the religious leadership, both parties to the alliance wanted to maintain it. The two leaderships would solve any problems that arose between them in the customary, Saudi manner: behind the scenes, quietly, calmly, at a measured pace, and leaving to time what could not be settled immediately.

From the first days of the crisis, the religious leadership stood resolutely behind the political leadership. It did not hesitate in permitting the request for the assistance of foreign forces, based on the principle of necessity. However, a group of preachers was not convinced by this position and disagreed with it. These preachers and missionaries thought it their religious duty to apply themselves to all matters equally, including details of ritual ablution and of foreign policy. Thus, the traditional division of labour between the political and religious leaderships became 'secularized', in the vein of 'render therefore unto Caesar what is Caesar's and unto God what is God's.' These preachers and missionaries criticized the foreign presence. Initially, the criticism was submerged and indirect. After the occurrence of the 'women's demonstration' (in which a group of Saudi women drove cars), which I will treat below, this criticism became an open attack against the state, which, in the view of the preachers, had become completely infiltrated by 'secularists'. Sermons were transformed into political analyses containing political criticism differing from the traditional criticism, which was limited to the media and soccer matches. A large number of preachers had obtained advanced degrees, and had even higher aspirations! Many also teach in the university. They viewed their role as being different from that of the traditional preacher, who was frequently a low-level employee with a limited education, and who was compelled to copy his sermons from an old book.

It would be an oversimplification to say that the politicized preachers in the Gulf were merely an echo of the Arab 'fundamentalist' movement. There was a clear difference. While this 'fundamentalist' movement supported the Iraqi president without reservation, the missionaries and preachers in the Gulf were attacking him fiercely, while also attacking, in a delayed reaction, the governments of the Gulf that had allied themselves with him. The occupation of Kuwait, according to this viewpoint, was nothing but divine punishment for sins, and especially the truce with 'heretical secularism'. However, if the preachers of the Gulf differed from the 'fundamentalist' movement with respect to premises, they did not differ from it in their insistence on rejecting the recourse to foreign forces. The consequence of both positions would have been the continuation of the occupation of Kuwait (until it was liberated by an army of Muslims!).

The 'fundamentalist' position, therefore, was in keeping with its final goal, which is the establishment of an Islamic state on the rubble of non-Islamic regimes. If non-fundamentalists view this position as opportunism which does not accord with the greatness of Islam, they should remember that man, throughout history, particularly political man, has always been able to use all means at his disposal in the service of a goal which he considers noble and honourable.

The 'fundamentalists' were not the only ones who saw the crisis serving their interests or achieving their goals. A large number of the Shi'a of the Gulf, who sympathized with Iran in the Iraqi–Iranian war, and who bear only enmity toward Saddam Hussein and the Gulf regimes that allied themselves with him during the war, viewed the crisis with satisfaction and malicious joy. In addition, nationalist, non-Shi'ite elements saw in the crisis the potential for the fall of the Iraqi Ba'ath party and of traditional regimes, which would permit the re-animation of the nationalist movement. Moreover, a number of persons living under Gulf regimes, including businessmen and intellectuals, hoped that the crisis would weaken these regimes and compel them to give a greater share of power to the groups to which they belong.

The heirs came to divide up the inheritance of the man who was still alive They came from all directions and were from every nation and creed. Strange things happened. Ba'athists fought against Ba'athists, while 'fundamentalist' Muslims stood with the secular heretic. Everyone attempted to divert the conflict to their benefit: the rich and the poor, the high and the low. The list of beneficiaries of the crisis even included a number of female drivers, those who staged a demonstration in Riyadh.

A number of Saudi women were of the opinion that the crisis provided the perfect climate for realizing an old dream, namely to drive a car. Everywhere there was talk of a new world order that respects human rights (including, without doubt, the right to drive a car!). In the kingdom there were now American female soldiers driving cars (and planes). The presence of hundreds of foreign journalists was tantamount to a guarantee that the government would agree to the women's demand for the right to drive. Actually, regarding the subject of women driving cars, the government had been yielding to public opinion rather than leading it. Public opinion in the kingdom, by a clear majority, does not support women driving cars (it also does not support women appearing in public with uncovered faces, and does not support women travelling without being accompanied by a close male relative).[1] These women, numbering close to 40, gathered near a large grocery store in Riyadh, sent their drivers away, and the 'women's demonstration' was launched.

None of the passers-by believed their eyes as they watched the women driving cars in the streets. No one knew how to act. The government itself was thrown into confusion, and the king was of the opinion that the matter should be left for the *ulema* to issue a formal legal opinion. Meanwhile, a dispute arose between the traffic police and personnel of the 'Organization for the Promotion of Virtue and the Suppression of Vice' regarding who had jurisdiction in dealing with these unprecedented violations. The dispute was settled with a compromise: the women were escorted to the police station in the presence of personnel of the organization. Hours later, the women were released after their husbands or relatives had signed a pledge stating that the violation would not recur.

The 'demonstration' led to great turmoil in conservative

[1] In the absence of precise statistics, anyone who so wishes can take issue with my remarks here about Saudi public opinion. I will be the first to acknowledge that what I have said is based solely on my personal impressions.

circles. Thousands massed around the office of Shaykh Bin Baz, who enjoys high standing among different classes of the Saudi people. The Shaykh issued a formal legal opinion prohibiting women from driving, and the Ministry of the Interior announced that it would resolutely apply that formal legal opinion. Matters quietened down. However, the politicized preachers viewed the demonstration as a 'secularist conspiracy'. It was impossible, in their view, that women would dare to undertake an insane act that challenged the values and traditions of society without a green light from the government. The 'women's demonstration' stimulated a wave of anger against the foreign presence, which had then begun to be seen as linked to 'secularism' inside the country. Cassette tapes were disseminated everywhere. They condemned the American female troops, the 'secular' Saudi female drivers, and anyone who sympathized with any of the demonstrators. In the view of the preachers Islam seemed to be besieged from all sides. There was the heretical secularist who had occupied Kuwait, the American female soldiers polluting the sacredness of the Arabian Peninsula with their presence, the 'Americanized' Saudi women who wanted to drive cars and 'Westernized' Saudi intellectuals. None of the preachers believed at the time, and perhaps would not now believe, that the government was as amazed by the 'demonstration' as were the relatives of the demonstrators who were summoned to the police station to sign a pledge.

Islam was thrust into the throes of the Gulf political crisis, even though no one studied Islam's texts in an unhurried, calm fashion in the light of the different aspects of the crisis to arrive at an 'Islamic judgment' on the issue. Each party adopted a political position based on political considerations, and justifications based on Islamic law came later. Those who opposed the invasion of Kuwait found texts to support their position. Those who welcomed the invasion found other texts. Each of the two parties selected those texts that accorded with its political position.

In the end, the 'fundamentalist' movement was unable to achieve its goals, despite the demonstrations, the cassette tapes and the preachers. Not one demonstration in sympathy with Saddam Hussein took place in the Gulf, and the hostility against the foreign presence was limited to a verbal attack.[1] However, the crisis proved that the 'fundamentalist' movement had become an important part of the Arab political reality, and that the battle which it lost was only 'a trial for what it will face' in the way of future battles.

[1]In the kingdom, a number of non-Saudis fired upon a truck filled with American soldiers, but no one was injured seriously. In Bahrain, a British soldier was stabbed by a mentally deranged person, and in Dubai, an Italian soldier was stabbed.

6

THE UNATTRACTIVE 'BEDOUIN' AND THE UGLY 'ARAB'

I suspect even those closest to me,
Knowing them to be human.

al-Mutanabbi

History has visited the Arabian Peninsula three times. The first was the advent of the message of Islam, the second was the appearance of a new, Salafiyah religious (reform) movement that became known, mistakenly, as 'Wahhabism', and the third was the discovery of oil. With the exception of these visits, the Arabian Peninsula has remained on the periphery of history. Were it not for the presence of the holy sites, those sites which every nation which ruled over the Islamic world has desired to control, the Arabian Peninsula would have been thrust even further into the margins of history.

With the departure of the fourth orthodox caliph from the city of Medina, the Arabian Peninsula was no longer the source of Islamic decision-making and has not become so again. This decision-making power has shifted between Baghdad, Damascus and Cairo. It has also moved between the capitals of North Africa and the metropolises of Arabicized Spain. It later returned to the east and the cities of Persia. It then settled in Istanbul. Culture – jurisprudence, poetry, science and philosophy – travelled with political decision-making. Throughout this rich history, the peninsula was merely a storehouse supplying the population required by the great Islamic armies. It was merely an unmined source of the 'Arab exotica' that fill literature. Anyone may peruse any book on Arab history and fail to find in it, with the exception of accounts of Mecca and Medina, more than a few paragraphs, that mostly concern rebel movements that were quickly suppressed.

There is no doubt that this historical legacy has created a highly sensitive relationship between inhabitants of the Arabian Peninsula and other Arabs (or between nomads and settled populations).[1] There is nothing to be gained from pretending that this sensitivity does not exist. During the crisis, when the Iraqi president began to refer to the countries of the Gulf Co-operation Council as 'bedouin', he was knowingly or unknowingly playing with highly combustible historical material.

From the viewpoint of the large Arab metropolises, the Arabian Peninsula, with the exception of Mecca and Medina, was a desert populated by savage, barbaric tribes, and anyone who made a pilgrimage to Mecca was highly apprehensive about the viciousness of these tribes, which remained outside any effective control. As a child today reads in bed stories of cannibalism, as he trembles in delicious fear, throughout history the child living in settled Arab areas has enjoyed the legends of the 'bedouin', beginning with the adventures of Antar, and ending with the 'bedouin' who lies in wait near the walls of the city to kidnap children of the settled population. The 'bedouin', who moves in the darkness and shadows and lives with the wolves and dwells in tents, acquired a legendary image that made him seem more like a demon than a human being. From the settled, urban outlook, the Prophet was a city-dweller who was able to spread his message despite the 'bedouins', not because of them. From this point of view, it has become imprecise to speak of the Arabian Peninsula as the birth-place of the Prophet's mission. That role is instead assigned to the two cities of Mecca and Medina.

If the Arabian Peninsula has lived in the shadows of history since the exodus of the orthodox caliphate, this is only natural in the view of urban Arabs. In the view of the urban population, Wahhabism was only a rebel movement, a mere 'bedouin' attempt to encroach on legitimate, urban power.

Needless to say, this urban outlook viewed the appearance of oil in the Arabian Peninsula as a heavy irony of fate. A prominent Arab official stated at one time that the presence of oil in the peninsula was merely a 'geological coincidence' which does not give the people of the peninsula any more right than other Arabs to the oil. The stupified peninsular officials listening to him remained silent. No one asked him

---

[1]Our discussion in this chapter reflects the general impressions, not the bare facts. The truth is that the bedouin (nomads) and the settled populations are located outside the Arabian Peninsula as well as inside it.

whether the 'geological coincidence' rule applied to all Arab resources, or was limited only to oil.

If anyone believes that the previous analysis contains some exaggeration, he need only refer to an article written by the most brilliant contemporary Arab journalist, Mohamed Heikal, in the London *Times* of 12 September 1990. In this article, the official spokesman for Nasirism expresses all of the sentiments of urban Arabs with extreme candour. Heikal states: 'The struggle for independence and ownership of the oil was waged from the cities of Cairo, Baghdad, Damascus and Beirut.' In Heikal's view, these cities represent the political centre of gravity and should have been the financial centre as well. Heikal adds: 'However, ultimately, it was the tribal leaders who obtained the oil and denied the cities the fruit of their [the cities'] labours.' We are presently not concerned with debating the accuracy of the designation 'tribal leaders', as much as with noting that Mr Heikal believes that the 'bedouin' acquired the oil of the 'settled' population without any right. It is only fair to say that the great journalist was bold enough to express a secret sentiment which pervades the hearts of residents of the large, Arab, urban centres, affecting both intellectuals and the general public.

This is how matters appeared to the 'settled population'. The 'bedouins', had an entirely different view that contains no coincidences. The population of the peninsula believes that God knows best where to place his message, and he did so in the Arabian Peninsula! 'Bedouin', as understood by the people of the peninsula, is a Quranic expression that refers to specific tribes which adopted a hostile attitude toward the Prophet's mission, and does not refer to all the Arabs of the peninsula, inasmuch as the 'bedouins' who are criticized in one place in the Holy Quran are praised elsewhere. The 'bedouins'' embracing of Islam was genuine, making them true Muslims regardless of their place of residence. The people of the peninsula believe that the Arab tribes in the peninsula were originally as hostile as the urban dwellers to the Islamic message and its army.

According to this outlook, it should come as no surprise that the most important reform movement in Islam in later ages should be based in the Arabian Peninsula, and that its banner should be carried by the people of the peninsula. If this movement appeared in the eyes of the urban Arabs as a minor rebellion originating in a small bedouin town, al-Dar'iyah, against the centres of decision-making and civilization in Cairo and Istanbul, it was, in the objective view of history the first intellectual shock to affect the Islamic world in centuries. It removed the Islamic world from the grip of superstition, heretical traditions, and Sufi dreams. The movement radiated smaller intellectual shock waves that reached Sudan, North Africa and India. It can be said, objectively, that the contemporary Islamic awakening has many historical roots of which the most important was the reform call witnessed by the Arabian Peninsula in the eighteenth century.

The people of the peninsula were extremely dismayed to see that the important intellectual role which their great reform revolution played was receiving no response from urban, Arab intellectuals, who ignored the pioneering model which the movement represented and which proves, in its practical application, that it is possible to establish a contemporary state on the basis of religion (despite the negative aspects necessarily entailed in any human effort). Until recently, 'Wahhabism' commonly meant extremism in belief and behaviour, and a boorish appearance. A senior Gulf official once told me 'Praise the Lord! When the kingdom adopted Islam it was "reactionary Wahhabism", and when Khomeini did the same, it became a "progressive revolution"!'

The pride of the people of the peninsula in their spiritual 'purity' can be noted throughout history. They feared the 'pollution' of the settled areas. In Najd, until recently (a time still recalled by the older generation), a person coming from the Gulf, where non-Muslims could be found, spent several days alone, without any visitors. In other words, he was placed in something resembling 'spiritual quarantine', until he could be purged of germs. Shaykh Shakhbut Bin Sultan, the previous ruler of Abu Dhabi, was extremely wary of 'Arabs' who would come to him from the Arab capitals, each one carrying proposals for new projects. He would repeatedly ask, 'why did you not come before?!' It was this same mentality of wariness toward foreigners and foreign influences that governed the behaviour of Sultan Sa'id Bin Taymur in Oman and Imam Ahmad in Yemen. Even to this day, some in the Arabian Peninsula wish that all foreigners, the good and the bad, would depart from the peninsula and leave it as it was before they came, before the discovery of oil!

If the people of the peninsula have believed that the appearance of Islam in the peninsula was not a concidence, and that the emergence of the Salafiyah reform movement in the peninsula was not a coincidence, they also believe that the discovery of oil in their peninsula was not a coincidence. They have suffered throughout history from hardships. They frequently died of hunger or were compelled by hunger to raid each other. They view the discovery of oil as a blessing bestowed by God, who provides means of subsistence to whomever he pleases. He singled them out because of their adherence to their creed and their long suffering under deprivation. Talk of a 'geological coincidence' is incomprehensible, let alone convincing.

The two views (that of settled society and that of traditional nomadic society) contradicted each other. In one corner stands the son of the peninsula who considers himself a soldier of Islam and the hero of genuine Arabism, who has continued to maintain the purity of his creed and ancient traditions, while the rest of the Muslims were prisoners of colonialism or decadence (or both). In the other corner stands the urban dweller, embodying the product of Islamic civilization in terms of thought and literature, who makes events and interacts with them, and who has only scorn for the nomadic bedouin who washes his hair in the urine of camels and aspires to lead the caravan of Islam. The two conflicting images could have continued to coexist peacefully owing to the lack of real contact betwen urban and bedouin populations, if it had not been for the advent of oil. Urban dwellers would have continued to ignore desert dwellers as they have done throughout most of history.

With the discovery of the largest oil fields in the world in the Arabian Peninsula, many very strange and disruptive developments have occurred. The tents went and the palaces came. Camels disappeared and Rolls-Royces came. The 'bedouins' who had until recently lived in the shadow of hunger came to possess legendary wealth. The centre of financial gravity (and political gravity) shifted from the metropolis to the desert. The Saudi used to go to Cairo and stand baffled in the face of what he saw there. Now the Egyptian would go to

Riyadh and not believe what he saw at the airport. Heads of major states were lining up to visit the 'tribal leaders' and obtain their approval. Palestinians, Syrians, Lebanese or Egyptians who had visited the peninsula as dear, honoured guests to teach the illiterates, provide them with medical treatment, or explain to them how to invest their money now came humbly to ask for work. The 'pre-oil' scenes differed amazingly from the 'post-oil' scenes, and the amazement in some cases turned into insanity.

The negative aspects are many, and it is easy to focus on them. How quickly we forget the positive aspects. It is in the nature of things that minor, daily events accumulate gradually in a way unnoticed by anyone. Suddenly, after many years, they explode in the form of a 'crisis', 'revolution' or 'war'. When that happens, researchers seek the direct causes and these are undoubtedly extremely important. However, the same researchers forget the long accumulation of history. Neglecting this history renders matters seemingly random. The image of the 'unattractive bedouin' in the mind of the settled population, and the image of the 'ugly Arab' in the eyes of the people of the peninsula were not created by Saddam Hussein. Nor are they results of the crisis. Rather, they are the outcome of numerous, minor, negative factors that have accumulated with time.

No one in the peninsula with a minimum measure of objectivity can deny that the behaviour of the people of the peninsula presents many negative aspects. There is no doubt that the rapidly acquired colossal wealth has led in many cases to a shameless decline in moral behaviour. 'Man abandons moderation if he becomes rich.' This is an eternal Quranic truth that existed before the discovery of oil and will continue to be true after the oil is exhausted. The bedouin of the peninsula, who until recently worked for food – i.e., he did not receive wages for his work and was compensated with food – now treats Arab 'labour' strangely. At the same time, no objective observer among urban Arabs would deny that the negative aspects are not limited to the 'owners of the oil'. Many who dealt with the Arabian Peninsula had a condescending attitude toward it, like this one expressed in a popular Egyptian story about a Turkish pasha who became impoverished and wandered about begging for charity, saying: 'Alms for the poor! I am your master!'

With the explosion of the Gulf crisis, people's internal feelings exploded. The Moroccan intellectual who could find no housing to shelter himself and his children applauded the army that would remedy this shortcoming (this position was of course swathed in a thick cloud of epistemological theorization behind which intellectuals almost always proceed). The Palestinian professional sympathized with the invasion because it promised to transform him from a hired worker (or slave) into a partner. The Tunisian journalist opposed the Gulf citizen, who was viewed in Tunisia only as an investor in projects from which he could make a quick profit, or a passing visitor who had no interest in the landmarks of Tunisian culture. Many of the demonstrators carried pictures of Saddam Hussein, but a great number of them were demonstrating against the image of the offensive bedouin!

In addition to the negative factors on both sides, there are objective facts which complicate the picture, and for which no one can be blamed. The Saudi soldier, for example, receives a salary that is much larger than that of a general in any non-oil Arab country. The income of a minor government official in Qatar or Abu Dhabi exceeds that of a minister in non-oil countries (our discussion is limited to legitimate income in both cases). In almost every Gulf home, there is at least one 'Asian maid'. When a Kuwaiti minister stated, following the crisis, that Kuwaiti families would in the future have to 'tighten their belts' and be satisfied with two maids, he caused a wave of ridicule in the Arab world. This income disparity is a fact of contemporary Arab life, as is the disparity between the income of a German citizen, which averages close to $20,000 a year, and that of a citizen of Bangladesh, which does not exceed $200. This is a fact of contemporary international life.

There is another historical objective fact concerning the history of colonialism in the Arabian Peninsula and in Arab metropolises. We must first remember that the heart of the Arabian Peninsula was never colonized (as was also the case in the mountains of Yemen and the mountains of Oman). The rest of the peninsula's territory was colonized only 'symbolically'. Even the Ottoman state, which controlled the Islamic world, exercised its rule only in the cities of the Arabian

Peninsula. Before oil, nothing in the Arabian Peninsula enticed any colonizer, whether Spanish, Portuguese, Dutch, French or British. The region was important only in so far as it was a part of the imperial communications network. Therefore, the colonizers were satisfied with exercising that measure of control which would keep the transport routes open to them but closed to others.

Whereas French settler colonialism was taking the form of a violent attempt to make the Arab Maghreb an inseparable part of France, members of the British government would have had a heart attack had anyone suggested to them making the Gulf an inseparable part of Great Britain. The British presence in the Gulf took the form of a political resident, a limited number of British officials, and a single warship whose presence made its use unnecessary. Until Nasirism began to spread its influence, the British presence in the Gulf did not encounter any significant resistance (unlike the British presence in Egypt, Palestine or Iraq). This presence was welcomed by local rulers, who viewed it as a guarantee of their independence in the face of a larger, more powerful neighbour. Moreover, this presence was sometimes welcomed by the rulers' subjects who viewed the British resident's proximity to the local ruler as a guarantee of their rights. While French colonialism was preoccupied with wiping out all landmarks of Islamic, Arab civilization in the Arab Maghreb, British colonialism in the Gulf was observing, with great enjoyment, local customs and asking his orientalists to document and record them!

With the advent of oil, the region was transformed into the most important strategic prize in the world. The colonial power began to treat the rulers with greater deference and respect (at least outwardly). For their part, the rulers welcomed companies coming from abroad to extract the treasures under the ground. Relations between the companies and the rulers, in the view of the rulers, seemed in keeping with their interests to a large degree. The delightful anecdote that circulated in the Gulf about that subordinate who told the shaykh that 'these are your English servants' describes the situation accurately – as it appeared to the subordinate. Would not the 'English' protect the shaykh from any external aggression? Would they not be preoccupied with extracting oil for him? Would anyone other than 'servants' carry out such tasks?!

The extreme sensitivity of many urban Arabs toward col-onialism or 'imperialism' is not as strong among the people of the peninsula. In the Kingdom of Saudi Arabia, for example, the Americans always felt compelled to respect the customs and traditions of the country. They had no special privileges, and the Islamic courts were authorized to hear any crimes which they committed.[1] The relationship between the Gulf governments and 'imperialism', regardless of our definition of 'imperialism', was not one of a gulf 'slave' to an American 'master', as some Arabs in the cities delight in imagining. Rather, it was a relationship of mutual benefits. The Americans dealt with these governments with extreme sensitivity, which was unknown in US dealings with the governments of the Arab countries with large cities. About three years before the Gulf crisis, King Fahd Bin ʿAbd al-ʿAziz strongly criticized the American ambassador to the kingdom in the presence of Phil-lip Habib, the envoy of the American president at the time. The US State Department immediately recalled the ambassador and then replaced him. It is doubtful whether an urbanized Arab country would dare treat the American ambassador as the bedouin country did.

Therefore, there are objective facts, and there are mental images, which are based partially on facts or which ignore them entirely, that have led to a 'dialogue of the deaf' between the bedouins and the settled populations and caused a confron-tation during the crisis. The people of the peninsula have awakened from a pleasant dream in which they starred as the darlings of the Arab world because of their wealth. They have discovered, as all rich people have discovered throughout his-tory, that money does not buy friends (and frequently buys enemies). The Arabs in the settled areas were surprised to find that the matter does not concern 'tribal leaders' who are in collusion with colonialism as much as the distinctive, gulf 'identity' of peoples who stood overwhelmingly with their governments, and who could not care less about the opinion of the 'progressive Arabs' or 'intellectual Arabs' on any matter. This requires review. Each party must begin such a review,

---

[1]Compare this situation to that in Iran, where every American citizen was given full diplomatic immunity. The attack by Ayatollah Khomeini against the law that granted this immunity in the early 1960s heralded the ascendance of his political star.

based on realism, which will enable it to appreciate and understand the historical problem and make it possible to overcome it. It is fair to say that the widespread image of the Gulf is not necessarily the correct image. Financial corruption in the Gulf in no way differs from financial corruption anywhere else in the Arab world (although the proportion might differ according to inflation!). The arrogant and wasteful attitude towards the blessings that accompany the oil wealth is the same as that which accompanies wealth of any kind. The Gulf governments have succeeded in developing the tribal, bedouin system, within which they have established the nucleus of a modern, advanced state. The achievements of development in the Gulf are not the making of propaganda agencies. Development in the Gulf is a tangible, extraordinary accomplishment that cannot be explained by wealth alone.

For example, there is the matter of women in Saudi Arabia. A third of a century ago, there was not a single school for girls. There are now more than 1.5 million female students. True, women do not drive cars in the kingdom. It is also true that, within the space of one generation, Saudi women have made the transition from being thought insane to demand education, to witnessing the graduation of tens of thousands of young women from the universities in various fields each year. All matters are relative, and the situation of women in the kingdom does not need to be compared with that of women in the United States or France. Rather, the situation of the contemporary Saudi woman should be compared with that of her mother or grandmother.

This amazing achievement in the field of education for women is repeated in all fields. Within a few years, the Gulf was able to build a welfare state that would have taken several centuries to build in the West. The aid and loans provided by the state to citizens reached the point where a number of Gulf economists were compelled to warn of the consequences of over-indulgence. Despite the real disparities of wealth, there was a tireless effort to channel oil revenues to every citizen. The result was that poverty, at least in its most extreme form, disappeared from most areas of the Gulf. It is doubtful whether any 'revolutionary' government would have been able to do more than the Gulf governments, whether in comprehensive development or the distribution of wealth.

The image of the 'tribal shaykh' who is an autocratic tyrant is closer to a political caricature than a reality. The king of Saudi Arabia, the ruler of Abu Dhabi, or the amir of Bahrain cannot order the execution of political opponents (although he can order their arrest), because religious considerations do not permit such behaviour. This is in contrast to the situation in a number of 'revolutionary' countries, where the 'protection of the revolution' permits the leader to undertake any measure to eradicate pests. No ruler in the Gulf can order the confiscation of the money, business or house of any citizen, because the inviolability of private property protects the citizen (unlike where socialism prevails). Rarely will a Gulf government take measures against a person's livelihood for political reasons whereas this is the first measure taken in a number of Arab countries.

No one should understand from these observations that I aim to depict ruling regimes in the Gulf as ideal or near to ideal. My only purpose is to emphasize that any comparison between these regimes and other Arab regimes would not be to the detriment of the Gulf. The fact of the matter is that if we wish to call things by their names, we would have to say that the entire Arab world is ruled by 'monarchies': individuals and their families govern for life. The difference between the Gulf and the other Arab countries is that the Gulf calls a 'kingdom' a 'kingdom', and surrounds it with a wall of traditional guarantees that are unavailable in non-traditional kingdoms, which are usually called 'republics'.

It is justified to stress that the people of the desert, though they are new to prosperity, have not neglected the performance of their national obligations. For example, the Kingdom of Saudi Arabia alone has provided foreign aid which, on the eve of the crisis, totalled close to $70 billion. Those who maintain that Gulf aid has not been provided in the correct manner forget that all methods have been tried, from development loans to direct gifts, the financing of arms deals, and joint projects. The Kuwaiti Fund for Arab Economic Development was a pioneering experiment in the Third World. Its method of operation was extremely precise and objective.

The people of the Arab cities are warmly invited, to rediscover the 'bedouins and sailors' in the peninsula and the Gulf. There is now a new world about which Arab intellectuals know almost nothing. Mr Heikal would no doubt be amazed – and perhaps incredulous – if we told him that the kingdom has young technocrats capable of managing the largest and most complex industrial projects which are not to be found elsewhere in the Arab world. There is no doubt that many Arab intellectuals would be amazed if they were provided with a list of the names of Gulf poets and writers. The bedouins have gone beyond being the repository of exotic lore!

If in these pages I wish to be as fair as possible, I must now shift my attention to the people of the Gulf. Every citizen of the Gulf should always remember that the Gulf population, including foreigners, does not exceed the population of Cairo (or double the population of Casablanca). Civilization is ultimately the outcome of numerous factors, of which the human factor continues to be the most important. If we were to divest the Gulf of its imported labour, all manifestations of life in the Gulf would cease immediately. Ironically, the news of the liberation of Kuwait was read on Kuwaiti television by a Palestinian broadcaster.

The people of the Gulf must liberate themselves from any 'delusions of grandeur' resulting from a feeling of power. The power which they currently enjoy derives from a single source that is being rapidly depleted. Throughout history, precious materials have guaranteed their possessor's temporary prosperity until they were replaced by other precious materials. In the beginning, there were spices and incense. Then came metals of various types, followed by rubber, cotton and finally oil. The current feeling of security in the Gulf is temporary, because it is linked to temporary wealth. The time has come to think about permanent security.

Permanent security requires of the people of the Gulf that they stop thinking according to the mentality of a closed 'club of the rich' and open themselves to the urban Arab centres, not with more money, but with more love and friendship. Housing problems in Egypt must be the concern of Gulf officials as much as Egyptian officials. The economic problems of the Moroccan people must not be left entirely on the shoulders of the Moroccan government. Aid does not have to be 'tribute' imposed on the party that provides it. Nor does it have to be mere 'charity' for the one who receives it. There is a big difference between co-operation between brothers and dealings between a rich donor and a destitute person. If the mentality of brotherhood prevailed at times, it was the kindness of the wealthy donor that appeared more often.

I want to say, briefly, that the 'unattractive bedouins' and the 'ugly Arabs' must approach each other to examine each other's traits with brotherly feelings. Each will discover that the attractions in these characteristics cover all ugliness.

7

AN AMERICAN CONSPIRACY OR A NEW WORLD ORDER?

Fear and safety are only
Figments of the mind.

al-Mutanabbi

The 'foreign conspiracy' theory is as old as human history. Throughout time, it has continued to retain its vitality and indeed it has become even more vigorous over the years. The advantage of such a theory is that it is exceedingly convenient. It meets with a favourable response from the public, and no one who believes in the 'foreign conspiracy' theory has to prove anything. No evidence has to be offered. It suffices to declare the existence of the conspiracy. An easy, convenient explanation is more acceptable to groups and individuals than one that is complicated and tedious.

This does not of course mean that there are no foreign conspiracies. Nor does it mean that anyone who embraces a foreign conspiracy theory is mistaken. There are, to be sure, foreign conspiracies. Some of them are the only possible explanation for certain events. However, a theory that attempts to explain everything as stemming from a conspiracy usually ends up not explaining anything. Those who speak of a conspiracy rarely explain its details and background, as if everything were obvious and without need of explanation.

While the 'American conspiracy' theory now prevails in the Arab world, there was a time when it was usually a 'British conspiracy'. Everything that happens or does not happen can be attributed to colonialism (or the 'servants of colonialism', which is President Jamal 'Abd al-Nasir's addition to the theory). There was a widespread saying in the Arab world at the height of British influence to the effect that the only reason why fish die in the sea and birds fall from the sky is British colonialism. The saying was not in jest. Then came the 'communist conspiracy'. Anyone who demanded a right or opposed a policy was immediately categorized by the government as a communist (even if such a person was a capitalist or a religious person who had never heard of Karl Marx). According to this theory, any demonstration in any Arab street was a communist demonstration, any publication distributed in the streets of an Arab capital was printed by the communist party, and any coup against an Arab government was organized by 'international communism'. With the retreat of British and Soviet influence, the atmosphere was cleared for the American theory, which became the 'mother of explanations' during and after the crisis.

This does not mean that we believe that the United States does not conspire. The Central Intelligence Agency was not established, and large sums of money and manpower were not allocated to it, to spread cultural influence throughout the world. Satellites were not placed in space to monitor soccer championships. Large intelligence monitoring centres were not deployed everywhere on the globe to eavesdrop on the prattle of the old women of the neighbourhood. Those who read these pages carefully will realize that I have accorded the American role in the crisis its real substantial dimension. I did so from a reading of American interests, without finding the slightest need to resort to a hidden and secret conspiracy.

My first objection to the 'conspiracy theory' is that it does not explain as much as it avoids explaining, and it poses more questions than it answers. Why did the United States conspire to occupy Kuwait and then conspire to liberate it? How could the American president become involved in a scheme that could possibly end with thousands of American deaths and the destruction of his presidency? Was the Iraqi president a partner in the American conspiracy? If he was a partner in it, does that make him a mere American agent? If he is not an American agent, what compelled him to allow himself to be carried away by the conspiracy? If the matter was entirely an American conspiracy, how do we explain the hesitancy of the American Congress, which permitted the use of force by a very small majority? If the goal of the conspiracy was to topple the Iraqi president, why did the battle stop where it stopped? If the goal was to destroy the Iraqi military machine, would it not have been more appropriate and safer to adopt the method of a blockade, which proved to be very effective in curbing the Iranian military machine? If the goal was to exhaust Gulf wealth, was it also necessary to exhaust other economies, including the American economy itself? How could the United States drag the entire world, including every major country, into its conspiracy?

The last question raises the second and most important reason for our objection to the conspiracy theory. This theory confers on the United States a mythical and extraordinary aura of absolute power that permits it to act freely throughout the world as if the entire globe were under its thumb. If the United States were able to order the Soviet Union, the Peoples' Republic of China, and the other major countries to become involved in its conspiracy, and all of these countries could do nothing but blindly follow the United States, what chance do the weak Arab countries have of resisting American influence? If the United States had such legendary power, would it not be the smart thing to attempt to coexist with it and its plans? The irony is that those who adopted the 'American conspiracy' theory consider themselves enemies of the United States, but their theory, contrary to their intention, leads to absolute submission to the United States.

The circulation of the 'American conspiracy' theory was facilitated by the fact that it started during the crisis in an international environment that seemed unusual and strange. Some were satisfied with it and others were not. Those who were pleased with the international situation, as it came to be revealed during the crisis, believed that this situation constituted an 'order', in the sense that it eliminated the chaos that prevailed before it. They maintained that this order was 'international' in the sense that the international community, which is represented by the United Nations, is the final arbiter in this order, and that it is 'new' in the sense that it points to a coming era in international relations that differs from any previous era. Those who are disturbed by the international situation believe that it is not an order but an hegemony, and that it is not international but American. They further believe that it is not new, but represents a return to the era of 'gunboat diplomacy'. The truth, as is usual with judgments of a political character, lies somewhere in between. There is not an entirely new international order but neither is the old international order entirely unchanged.

Since international society began to emerge in its present form, which began with the breakup of feudalism and the appearance of the nation state in the seventeenth century, and lasted until the end of the Second World War, international relations have been governed by an order known as the 'balance of power'. This balance is between major countries, which number, in most cases, no less than five but rarely as many as ten. A 'balance of powers' in its simplest definition is a tireless attempt to prevent any state or number of states from extending their political hegemony over other countries. The wars witnessed by humanity since that time, including the Second World War, have been nothing but attempts to overturn the balance countered by efforts to restore it.

With the end of the Second World War, the major victors – the United States, the Soviet Union, Britain, France, and China – decided to clothe 'the balance of power' in the garment of 'collective security'. The allies produced the United Nations Charter, which made the Security Council the agency responsible for the stability of international society. The major countries granted themselves the right of permanent membership of the Security Council. They also granted themselves the right to veto any decision that affects their interests. In other words, the five major countries combined to create a police station to impose respect for order on the residents of the global neighbourhood.

In order for the police station to operate as planned, a mutual understanding had to be reached among its members. The five countries assumed that they would behave in the post-war period with the same friendly spirit that governed the alliance during the war. However, matters did not proceed in this way. As soon as the United Nations began operating, it discovered that fate had a bitter surprise in store. The 'balance of power' order which the United Nations and its Security Council had produced disappeared to be replaced by a new, strange order previously unknown to the world, namely an order based on two superpowers. Under the new order, the 'balance' was no longer between a group of major countries, but was limited to two countries, which became transformed from major powers into superpowers – the United States and the Soviet Union. Shortly thereafter, this balance between the superpowers turned into the 'cold war', which threatened from time to time to turn into an atomic war that would leave nothing behind.

The choice facing the other countries of the world was clear. They had either to join the Western bloc, join the Eastern bloc, or remain neutral, albeit, regardless of what was said about "positive neutrality", aligned with one of the two blocs. That which infuriated one superpower gladdened the heart of the other, and vice versa. A number of 'neutral' leaders enjoyed obtaining as much as possible from each of the two blocs. Such a leader did so by hinting that he or she was preparing to join the other bloc. The cold war crept into the Security Council and paralysed it. The police station was no longer able to carry out its security duties, because the policemen had split into two blocs.

The system of two superpowers did not change suddenly with the Gulf crisis. Complicated international systems do not collapse overnight. The causes of the gradual collapse of the order based on two superpowers had been undermining it slowly for years. The two superpowers had begun to realize that the cold war had reached an impasse, and a reconciliation or something like it began to replace it. Then the frightening economic weakness that transformed the Soviet Union from a superpower into a mere major power became apparent, although it maintained its military superiority and nuclear teeth, which many commentators disregard. Then the winds of change began to blow over the countries of Eastern Europe, removing the yoke of communist rule and ending subordination to the Soviet Union. Finally, a new type of giant, an economic giant in the form of Japan and a united Germany, entered the picture. In short, the world order was restored to a 'balance of power' and harmony returned among the major countries. The Security Council was thus able to play the role stipulated for it by the United Nations Charter.

The Iraqi president did not understand these changes. His behaviour continued to be governed by the cold war doctrine, according to which it suffices to announce a 'battle' against the United States to drag in the Soviet Union. Saddam Hussein was surprised when matters did not proceed in this way. He was surprised by the Security Council acting with great effectiveness unprecedented in its entire history (with the exception of the position of the Security Council during the

Korean crisis, which it was able to adopt because the Soviet Union temporarily withdrew from its proceedings). Perhaps the Iraqi president still, even now, is unable to understand 'the perfidy' of the Soviet Union.

This therefore is the 'new world order'. It is not based on total American hegemony as imagined by some. Nor is it the dawn of an era of shining justice anticipated by others. This order is a detente between a group of major countries, including giants, quasi-giants and economic giants, no more and no less. The new order is like the one that preceded it and the order that will follow it. It is neither for nor against the Arabs. This order contains as many opportunities as it does dangers for the Arabs and others. The United States plays a role in this order that is no smaller and perhaps greater than the role it played in the old order. Therefore, it is necessary to take a realistic view of Arab–American relations.

Arab hostility toward the United States stems primarily from a single cause, which is America's unstinting support for Israel. If we assume for the purpose of argument that this bias toward Israel were suddenly to change, all Arab feelings of hostility towards the United States, or most of them, would change with equal speed. No one can truly understand this position unless he understands what Palestine means to every Arab. Just as it is difficult for non-Jews to imagine the Jewish psyche after the Holocaust in Nazi Europe, it is difficult for non-Arabs to imagine the effect of the loss of Palestine on the Arab psyche. It suffices here to say that all major factors in Arab political life have in one way or another been bound up with the problem of Palestine.

Following the Arab military defeat of 1948, a wave of military coups began in the Arab world. The true goal behind these coups, regardless of their declared goals, was to remove the shame of the defeat. The enormous popularity of President Jamal 'Abd al-Nasir in the Arab world did not stem from his social achievements as much as from his appearance to be the only Arab leader capable of challenging Israel. Moreover, the Arab cold war which divided the Arabs for a long time into 'revolutionary' and 'reactionary' camps was not based on an analysis of the domestic policies in each country as much as on an assumed conception of each country's position on the problem of Palestine. The prevailing view at the time maintained that the 'revolutionary' countries alone would liberate Palestine, whereas the 'reactionary' countries were, because of their links with 'colonialism', unable to participate in the liberation. The slogan at the time asserted that the road to Palestine must pass through Sanaa or Riyadh, meaning that a revolution aimed at the liberation of Palestine was needed in every part of the Arab world.

What non-Arabs do not know is that the problem of Palestine, in addition to its physical aspect of the expulsion of an Arab people from its homeland and the replacement of Palestinian refugees by foreigners, acquired a symbolic, emotional dimension with immense power to unleash Arab feelings. The Palestine problem became a symbol of all that is desirable and all that is hated. It became a symbol of Arab weakness in the face of Israeli power. It became a symbol of Arab shame in the face of Israeli arrogance. It became a symbol of Arab backwardness compared with Israeli sophistication. The confrontation with Israel was no longer merely a border dispute or political conflict. It became a conflict with all that is repulsive in the Arab reality. A victory over Israel no longer entailed a military triumph decided by the quality of arms and leadership. Rather, it required a spiritual struggle to overcome all tendencies toward weakness and capitulation in the Arab psyche.

With its military and political superiority, Israel became a permanent insult to Arab honour. It was inconceivable for 100 million Arabs to accept, psychologically, that a small state of several million could be an enemy whom it was impossible to defeat. It was necessary to transfer the responsibility to 'those behind Israel', i.e. the United States. The facts of American support for Israel made this psychological justification possible and logical. The conflict actually became a conflict with the United States, and Israel became a mere catspaw, a mere agent of American imperialism. In this way, slogans hostile to the United States achieved the same magical effect in the psyche of the masses as anti-Israel slogans.

Many Arabs outside the Gulf were surprised by the effective military co-operation between the United States and the Gulf countries throughout the crisis. These Arabs did not see that the occupation of Kuwait had become the primary problem with Palestine taking a back seat. The same factors that made the Arabs hate Israel made the Gulf Arabs hate Saddam Hussein. With the return of Kuwait to normalcy, the Palestinian issue would return to its pivotal position among Arab causes. However, this cause had continued over the years to be a victim of gross mishandling. If progress is desired in the coming phase, the mishandling must end. This requires that the Palestinians themselves make three critical decisions which they should have made long ago.

The first is to decide that the Palestinian leadership will speak with a single voice. Pluralism is a blessing in countries, but a curse in revolutions. The Palestinian revolution is perhaps the first pluralistic revolution in all history. Every revolutionary movement which is divided into parties is compelled to form a collective leadership that necessarily becomes the 'coalition government', with all that characterizes such governments in changes of course and slowness of reaction. The Palestine problem – starting with the chronic conflict between the al-Husseini family and the al-Nashashibi family during the British mandate, and ending with the different 'parties' and 'organizations' which currently exist – has always had a multiplicity of spokesmen. There is a nationalist current, an Iraqi Ba'athist current, a Syrian Ba'athist current, a Marxist current, and an Islamic current. Each current speaks on behalf of the Palestinian cause and imposes its own priorities.

The final result of the existence of all of these political contradictions is that the function of leadership becomes a constant attempt to adhere to the lowest common denominator. In these circumstances, the 'leader' is transformed from a person capable of leading to one with whom all the parties are satisfied out of fear of a worse alternative. The leader becomes a sentimental, patriarchal symbol (see my remarks above on the emotional aspect of Yasir 'Arafat's personality). In these circumstances, the desirable characteristics of leadership – courage, wisdom, the ability to make difficult decisions – disappear. They are replaced by the characteristics desirable in a party leader – compliancy, the ability to arrange compromises, and day-by-day dealings with events. I believe that the current Palestinian leadership would be the last to deny that it is only too easy for it to function as a party leadership.

The second crucial decision awaiting the Palestinians is finally and conclusively to extricate their cause from the quagmire of Arab disputes. For fifty years, the Palestinians have been involved, sometimes intentionally and sometimes under compulsion, in every Arab dispute, with tragic results. The alignment of the current Palestinian leadership with the Iraqi president, even if it is unprecedently short-sighted, remains a mere symptom of the malady of involvement in Arab political entanglements. The time has come for the Palestinians to realize that – the Arab order being what it is, their cause being what it is, and their opponents being who they are – they, the Palestinians, will ultimately be the biggest loser. Perhaps the current crisis is the best proof that this is the truth. At the end of the crisis, each country settled down within its borders, with its sovereignty, and with its people. Only the Palestinians remained in the wilderness.

The third decision, which is the most important, is to adopt a clear, definitive position on whether to pursue war or peace. Anyone who speaks of war as he prepares for peace, or who speaks of peace as he prepares for war, or who speaks one day of war and the next of peace, might obtain a temporary media advantage. However, in the long term, he loses credibility regarding either option. This is precisely what has happened to the current Palestinian leadership. Over a quarter of a century, Yasir 'Arafat and his comrades have been speaking about peace in international organizations and about war in the refugee camps. The international organizations believe what is said to the refugee camps, and the refugee camps believe what is said to the international organizations. The schizophrenic nature of the Palestinian position has embarrassed all of the Palestinians' friends, while their enemies have focused on the talk of war and have neglected the talk of peace. They have succeeded in depicting the PLO as a bloodthirsty terrorist organization. The PLO has failed to reap the fruits of its making peace, and it has also failed to reap the fruits of its making war. In the previous chapter, we saw how the frustration that followed this failure – and frustration alone – was responsible for the PLO's alignment with Saddam Hussein in the Kuwait adventure.

Regardless of whether the final Palestinian decision, and the Arab decision following it, is to make war or to make peace, it would be advisable, when making this decision, to remember that Israel does not have colossal and invincible power. If, before the Six Day War, the Arabs made the fatal mistake of underestimating Israel's strength, a number of Arabs, after that war, have made the equal mistake of inflating Israeli power, depicting it as invincible. The Arabs tend to forget that, during the 1973 war, the Israeli prime minister thought of resigning and the Israeli defence minister thought of suicide. Two Arab states were able to stage a surprise attack against Israel, the implications of which continue to remain unknown to date. More recently, the youths of the *intifada* have been able to attract the world's attention by facing the Israeli military machine for three years with only stones in their hands.

If we believe that absolute American hegemony over the world is an illusion, we must also believe that there is no Israeli hegemony in this world. The Zionist movement succeeded in exploiting the international sympathy that followed the Holocaust in Europe. It succeeded in building an effective lobby in a number of influential countries, and it managed to create an effective military force. That is all. Nothing prevents the Arabs from creating international sympathy for the Palestinian cause (something of this sort happened during the *intifada*). Nothing prevents the Palestinians from forming an Arab lobby to neutralize the activity of the Israeli lobby. Nothing prevents them from building a military force to balance Israeli power.

Throughout the crisis, the US government continued to speak of a new international order and of the rights of small countries. Such talk, regardless of whether or not it is sincere, undoubtedly placed upon the United States, in the eyes of the international community, an obligation to promote Palestinian rights as it promoted Kuwaiti rights. All indications show that the US government now considers arriving at a solution to the Middle East problem its greatest priority after this had been a marginal concern since the end of the Arab oil boycott against the United States following the 1973 war. Whenever the United States pursues a solution to the crisis, signs of disagreement between the United States and Israel emerge. The Arabs must be ready this time to exploit this disagreement.

The American partiality for Israel was not created by historical, geographical, political or economic facts. It is entirely the creation of the Israeli lobby in the United States. The American political system, regardless of whether we view it as good or bad, remains open to pressure groups, both domestic and foreign. Effective foreign lobbies operate in the United States. In addition to the Israeli lobby, there is a Greek lobby, a Polish lobby, an Irish lobby, and an Armenian lobby – which have succeeded in operating effectively. It is worth mentioning here that the influence of the Zionist lobby in the United States is not an eternal, constant fact. It is currently facing several problems. The number of Jews in the United States is continuously declining as the result of intermarriage. They now number 4.3 million (1.8 per cent of the population). This decline has begun to raise fears in the Jewish community regarding the possible decline of Jewish influence. At the same time, the Zionist lobby is facing growing difficulties in collecting contributions from Jews due to the disappearance of the generation that experienced the Nazi mass killings and the birth of Israel.[1]

In the mid-1970s, the Kingdom of Saudi Arabia sent a delegation to the United States comprising a number of university professors, media persons and businessmen (some of whom had studied in the United States). The delegation spent several weeks in different American cities, meeting with different groups active in American society. The Zionist B'nai B'rith organization was dismayed by the success achieved by the delegation. The organization wrote an entire book on the delegation's activities, at the end of which it states that this delegation was the first successful Arab media offensive in the United States. It is extremely unfortunate that neither the kingdom nor other Arab countries have repeated this attempt.

The former Iraqi ambassador in Washington, Dr Nazzar Hamdun, and the current Saudi ambassador in Washington, Prince Bandar Bin Sultan, have succeeded in achieving a degree of political effectiveness which no Israeli ambassador has been able to achieve. If these two Arab ambassadors have necessarily focused on bilateral relations, they could also have focused on a single Arab plan, if it existed, and extend Arab achievement. This emphasises that the door is wide open to the Arab countries to exercise the same influence in the American political arena as Israel does.

This writer believes that the key to a solution is ultimately in the hands of the Arab countries, and not necessarily in Washington. American decision-makers, like all decision-

[1] See *Newsweek* magazine, no. 22, July 1991, p. 54.

makers, deal with reality as they perceive it. The reality currently perceived is one of Israeli military and political superiority.[1] If American support played a role in this superiority, inter-Arab disagreements played no less and perhaps more of a role. The Israelis themselves are, of all people, most aware of this fact. They have been admirably skillful in exploiting Arab differences and in depicting them as an inseparable part of Arab political life.

Israeli military superiority is a direct result of the split in Arab military ranks. Even after Iraq's temporary exit from the military equation, any comparison between Israel's military strength and Arab military strength would not favour Israel. If we combine all Arab missiles, aircraft and tanks, we find that they surpass what Israel has. The profound realization of this fact by Israeli leaders has led them to seek security in nuclear weapons. Even these weapons seem limited in their effectiveness in the face of the Arabs' manpower and strategic depth. If Iraq had headed west instead of south, it would have been able by itself to place Israel before its greatest challenge since its birth.

It remains to say that there is a significant dualism in the Arab position on the United States. There is a collective Arab position of opposition to the United States because of its partiality to Israel. Then there is an individual Arab position that is based on a fine calculation of narrow, individual interests. If a number of Arabs outside the Gulf disapproved of the Gulf countries' position on the United States during the crisis, the Gulf countries noted that not one Arab country severed its relations with the United States (except Iraq). While the Gulf people were facing the most severe rebukes because of their friendship with the United States, every other Arab government was seeking to strengthen its bilateral relations with the United States!

The dualism in dealing with the United States applies to individuals as well as to states. During the crisis, a Saudi friend encountered a Pakistani physician living in Los Angeles. The friend heard the Pakistani deliver a lecture in which he

[1]Dr Brzezinski, in 1980, when he was the national security adviser to President Carter, told me bluntly: 'What do you Arabs expect the United States to do for you after Israel defeated you on the battlefield?!' My response was: 'If only you would say this in public!'

chided the kingdom for being lax with respect to its religion and traditions in allowing American forces to use Saudi territory. The physician stated that these forces would bring with them all the physical and spiritual diseases of American society, especially AIDS. After the physician finished the lecture, my Saudi friend asked him why he left his Islamic country, especially when his country needs his medical services urgently, and why he emigrated to America to live in its corrupt society. Naturally the physician's response was total silence. A large number of Arab intellectuals who attack the United States day and night own houses in the United States that are ready to receive them when needed, i.e. if their attacks against the United States cause them to emigrate to the United States! Some of those who attacked the American position throughout the crisis are Arabs who have American citizenship.

One can love the United States to the point of being blind to its defects and shortcomings. The late President Anwar Sadat was afflicted with such love, which compelled him to repeat his famous, erroneous statement: '99 per cent of the cards are in America's hand.' One can also loathe the United States in an all-consuming hatred. However, love and hate, which are natural emotions in a romantic relationship, are ridiculous in relations between countries. The true challenge is not whether we love or hate the United States. The true challenge is to analyse our interests calmly and realistically, and to pursue our interests, whether they take us towards friendship with the United States, or towards hostility towards it, or – and this is most likely – towards agreement with some of its policies and opposition to others.

8

THE FUTURE: DIALOGUE OR EXPLOSION

All of us are perfect;
Who is to blame then?

al-Mutanabbi

In the midst of the crisis, several weeks before Desert Storm began, when the entire world was asking whether the crisis would end peacefully or in war, King Hasan II, the Moroccan monarch, spoke eloquently and effectively before the Moroccan parliament about the crisis and its developments. The Moroccan monarch concluded his speech by urgently cautioning the Iraqi president about the consequences of a military confrontation, which would end not only with the destruction of the Iraqi military machine, but also with Iraq's return to the period of 'the mandate'.

The days passed, the storm blew, and the Moroccan king's prophecy was realized as Iraq entered a mandate period. However, perhaps the Moroccan monarch was somewhat cautious, because the situation in Iraq following the war is much worse than the situation that existed during the mandate, when Iraq enjoyed the outward trappings of sovereignty and some of its substance. No military plane can take off in Iraq without permission. Iraq was compelled to acknowledge publicly that it robbed and plundered Kuwait. It had to pledge publicly to return what it stole. A large area of northern Iraq has been removed from the central government's control and declared a 'security zone' for the Kurds.[1] Most importantly, Iraq has agreed to destroy its missiles and chemical, biological and nuclear weapons. Moreover, it has announced its willingness to 'fully co-operate' in this regard. If the Iranian leader, Ayatollah Khomeini, had considered his consent to a cease-fire tantamount to swallowing a cup of poison, the Iraqi president was

[1] Recently a 'no-fly zone' in the south was added to protect the Shi'a from air attacks.

139

forced to swallow all of his 'binary chemicals' following the cease-fire resolution after Desert Storm.

Many were hoping that Saddam Hussein would die a martyr during the battle and enter history as a legend of defiance and resistance. Many had hoped that the Iraqi president would leave the stage and place his onerous legacy on the shoulders of one of his colleagues. However, Saddam Hussein disappointed all these hopes. He demonstrated that his desire to die as a martyr is weaker than his desire to withdraw. The Iraqi president was able to quell the rebellion in the south, end the rebellion in the north, and keep all the strings of power in his hand. Saddam Hussein was content to return as a survivor from his adventure in Kuwait. However, staying alive in a regime such as Saddam Hussein's requires staying at the apex of power. He is aware of this fact, as are all his friends and enemies.

The means used by Saddam Hussein to remain in power are the same means which have proved their effectiveness in the past. The Iraqi president went back twenty-five years to resurrect the same schemes that were used effectively in the early 1970s. The idea of a 'front' which rules Iraq, in which the Ba'ath Party is but one of a number of members, re-emerged under the name of 'pluralism'. The idea of 'autonomy' for the Kurds returned in full force without any appreciable change, whether implied or explicit (the only change is that the principle Kurdish negotiator is the son of the previous Kurdish negotiator). Normal relations were restored with Iran following the restoration of the 1975 Algiers Agreement on the same old basis: the division of the Shatt al-Arab.

Saddam Hussein is betting that he will succeed this time as he did the last time. 'Pluralism' constitutes a temporary phase, after which the Ba'ath Party will return to exclusive power.[1] Autonomy for the Kurds will remain as long as Iraq is subject to the international mandate. The Shatt al-Arab will remain divided as long as Iraq is militarily incapable of reclaiming it in its entirety. Through these manoeuvres, Saddam Hussein is betting that he will remain Iraq's absolute ruler until he dies (preferably of natural causes!).

Although we know that all who have spoken of the immi-

[1]A year after Desert Storm Saddam Hussein announced that Western-style democracy was not suitable for Iraq.

nent end of Saddam Hussein have been forced to swallow every word that they said, I none the less believe that there is a political law that prevents him from continuing to remain in power. This law stipulates that every army that suffers a crushing defeat must seek a political scapegoat to bear full responsibility for the defeat. Nothing makes us believe that Iraq's army will deviate from this rule, especially given that this army did not participate in any way in the decisions that led to the defeat (although it is said that a number of senior officers warned Saddam Hussein that the military confrontation would result in a disaster). It suffices in this regard to recall that, after the 1948 defeat, Arab armies toppled a number of Arab regimes, and, after the June 1967 war, the Syrian army carried out a 'corrective measure operation' that removed the government. Also, the Egyptian army was on the verge of imposing its will on President Jamal 'Abd al-Nasir (who thwarted the attempt by appealing to the masses directly). As long as the Iraqi president remains in power, there is no hope of normalizing relations between Iraq and the countries of the coalition, of forging new relations between Iraq and its neighbours, or of the lifting of the severe sanctions that have been imposed on Iraq (the sanctions are no doubt an additional factor that strengthens the effectiveness of the 'law of the defeated army' in its application to Saddam Hussein). Press reports coming out of Baghdad after the war do indeed point to a number of military attempts to dispose of Saddam Hussein, and it is doubtful that he will remain able to thwart them.

In Jordan, with peerless political skill, King Hussein has completely reversed his tendency to go along with the invasion of Kuwait. The king dissolved the government that was running the country during the crisis and appointed a new prime minister. He also declared a new national charter that allows political pluralism (i.e. that cancels the privileged position which the fundamentalist movement had enjoyed). King Hussein was the first ally of the Iraqi president to realize that the adventure in Kuwait had ended in a devastating failure. He was also the first Iraqi ally to decide to cut his losses by renouncing the originator of the adventure. In July 1991, an American journalist asked the Jordanian king his opinion on the resignation of Saddam Hussein. The king responded, very diplomatically, that, personally, he would resign if he found himself in the same situation. With these fast moves, King Hussein guaranteed that any attempt to restore the status quo would start with Jordan, and with him personally.

In Palestinian circles, there began, for the first time, public criticism of the leadership's full alignment with Iraq, which led to the Palestinians' complete isolation after the crisis. Even though these criticisms did not succeed in unseating the Palestinian president or in undermining his position, they demonstrated the existence of a growing rift in the Palestinian consensus which Yasir 'Arafat had previously taken for granted. It began to be rumoured that a 'new government' would assume responsibility for dealing with the post-crisis reality. Regardless of whether this government emerges, the Palestinian leadership must acclimatize itself to the circumstances that have developed in the wake of the failed adventure if it wishes to exercise any influence in the Arab arena.

In Tunisia, the honeymoon between the government and the 'fundamentalist' movement ended violently with arrests, expulsions and a charge of a conspiracy to overthrow the ruling regime. In Algeria, on the eve of general elections, the government announced that the 'fundamentalist' movement was seeking to seize power directly. It arrested a number of the movement's leaders, and the Algerian army assumed responsibility for maintaining security under existing laws. In Yemen, there were continuous strikes that paralysed activity in a number of sectors. In Sudan, the government clashed with students at Khartoum University, and many doubts were raised about its ability to survive. In Mauritania, the government announced a new constitution that opened the way for a new phase in political pluralism.

The 'storms after the storm' were not limited to Iraq and its allies. The winds of change blew everywhere. In Saudi Arabia, during the crisis, a number of intellectuals and businessmen prepared a letter to King Fahd asking for the establishment of a consultative council and the expansion of the range of personal freedoms. Before the letter was submitted, the king preempted events by announcing, in November 1990, his intention to declare a basic law of government and statutes for a consultative council after the crisis had ended. In more than one public speech, the king stressed that the time had come to conduct a comprehensive review that would cover 'everything', i.e. all organizations and all laws.

The king was therefore extremely dismayed when a new petition was presented to him signed by about 400 people, most of whom work in jurisprudence and the Islamic universities. The petition was written in extremely sharp language and included twelve demands. Behind all these demands was the main, unwritten demand, which is for the placing of different state activities at home and abroad under the control of authorized legal (Islamic law) committees. There was nothing unusual in a group of judges and university professors putting forth demands. There had already been one petition (even if it had not been submitted) as well as the 'women's demonstration'. If the 'liberals' had expressed their demands candidly, there was nothing to prevent the 'conservatives' from expressing their views as well. What was provocative was that the petition was put forward with the blessing of major clerics in the core of the religious leadership, namely Shaykh ʿAbd al-ʿAziz Bin Baz and Shaykh Muhammad al-ʿAthimiyah. The first question that immediately springs to mind is: has the relation between the religious and political leaderships changed? The question is will each of these two leaderships carry out their legal functions in isolation from each other? The Organization of Senior Ulema promptly convened a meeting that was attended by Shaykh Bin Baz and Shaykh al-ʿAthimiyah. The meeting resulted in the issue of a communiqué that openly criticized the way in which the petition had been circulated, as if it were a political leaflet. It also implicity criticized the style of its contents, which focussed on negative factors and ignored positive factors. Whatever the wording of the communiqué, its objective was to make clear that the relation between the two leaderships had not changed at all. The situation quietened down in expectation of the king's announcement of the constitution, which he made in March 1992.[1]

With the promulgation of the basic law of government the kingdom has taken an important step towards creating a constitutional framework for broad changes that Saudi society witnessed in the late 1960s, when decisions were taken to abolish slavery, provide education for women, and introduce

[1]These elections, held in October 1992, produced a parliament with a majority of opposition figures, thus presaging a potential constitutional crisis.

143

television – resolutions which amounted to a major social revolution. In the mid-1970s, when the Saudi government decided that it would begin the biggest development process witnessed by any Arab country, and perhaps by any country in the world, it decided on a second social revolution. It is illogical that such immense social change would occur in the absence of accompanying intellectual and political changes.

In Oman, Sultan Qaboos hastened to change the appointed consultative council into a semi-elected council that is to enjoy very different powers from the merely formal powers of the old council. Throughout the entire Gulf, people were waiting to see what the constitutional changes in the kingdom would lead to. However, the real interest in the Gulf was focussed on the events in Kuwait.

It was unreasonable to expect that the Kuwaiti government, which returned following a violent occupation lasting several months, would be able to solve all outstanding problems overnight. The strong desire for revenge against those who collaborated with the occupier, which affect any state that is liberated, also arose in Kuwait. In the first days following the liberation, atrocities occurred that were only ended when the Kuwaiti crown prince openly threatened to hang anyone who continued this type of retaliation. At first, the government was struck by semi-paralysis in dealing with the heavy legacy of the occupation, which included the burning oil wells and inoperable water and electricity utilities. However, these expected problems, which began to be handled more effectively with time, were not the main source of concern. The focus was on developments in the political arena.

The dispute between the government and the opposition in Kuwait is as old as the constitution that was declared with independence and the inauguration of democracy as the method of government. Such a dispute would usually be settled by friendly means. However, it twice came to a head, once in the 1970s and once in the 1980s, in a way that led to the dissolution of the elected National Assembly. During the crisis, the government and the opposition agreed to the return of this assembly. However, the agreement apparently did not provide for the return of the old, disbanded assembly immediately upon the liberation of Kuwait; the government saw fit to call for new elections to be held in the autumn of 1992.

What is happening now in Kuwait is a microcosm of the painful process of change that is occurring throughout the Arab world. All political currents in the Arab arena are reflected in one way or another in Kuwait arena, where the number of 'tendencies' and 'blocs' exceed the number of fingers on both hands. The Kuwaiti experiment is an Arab 'laboratory', and the success or failure of the experiment in pluralism in Kuwait will be an indication of its success or failure throughout the rest of the Arab world. The problem of pluralism in Kuwait is the same as that throughout the Arab world: there are no clear rules governing democracy which are acceptable to everyone.

'Democracy' means different things to the Kuwaiti government and opposition. From the government's standpoint, the entire constitution, with all of its democratic principles, was a 'gift' from the amir, and it is unreasonable and unacceptable for the gift to be turned against the donor. Democracy, based on this premise, means cooperation between the amir and the elected body, whose, rules and dimensions are determined by the amir, not the elected body itself. On the other hand, to the opposition democracy means the rule of the people; if there is a conflict between the body elected by the people and the government (which is not elected), the elected body shall have the final say. This difference between the outlook of the government and that of the opposition is the natural outcome of the absence of parameters within which the game of democracy is played. What is this democracy which has begun to 'spread through the world and preoccupy the people'?

There are numerous words – 'plurality', 'democracy', 'consultation' – that refer to the same phenomenon, which means, at the least, the expansion of the base of political participation, and, at the most, a government which is elected by the people. In all cases, it means the existence of constitutional guarantees that limit the ruler and protect the rights of the ruled. This phenomenon has constituted, since the late 1980s, the wave of the future. Democracy has not always enjoyed this position, and it is not certain that it will continue to occupy it in the future.[1] Historical developments do not unfold in a straight line. Every victory is subject to a setback. However, it is clear

[1]Had the August 1991 coup in the Soviet Union succeeded it would have been a severe setback for democracy.

that democracy is currently the historical influence from which all winds of change will issue.[1] When any phenomenon becomes a 'historical influence', it obtains great momentum that is extremely dangerous, and perhaps impossible, to resist.

Many now calling for pluralism in the Arab world are not doing so as a matter of principle, but out of a desire to expand the scope of their influence. A 'fundamentalist' cleric, who takes up 'consultation' as a weapon against a government which he opposes politically, calls anyone who opposes him politically an unbeliever. A businessman who calls for democracy is in fact demanding a greater role in political decision-making. The intellectual who wants elections will be the first to attack elections if he loses in them. None the less, the rules of the democratic game do not stipulate that every party must be free of selfish interests. This game is based on permitting different interests to compete for the votes of an electorate.

The primary political problem of the Arab world is that the democratic game is not played according to well-known rules, simply because there is not a single democratic government in the Arab world. It is difficult, if not impossible, for a government that has not been elected to move toward democracy. All Arab regimes can be divided into those that attained power through hereditary legitimacy and those that attained it through revolutionary legitimacy. Needless to say, no regime would voluntarily renounce the legitimacy it acquired when it came to power, and leave its fate to elections whose outcome would be unknown.

Throughout the entire Arab world, non-democratic governments are being called upon to become democratic immediately. Such immediacy might occur in stories or movies, but not in the reality of politics. History tells us that political reform is accomplished in only two ways: gradual, slow change or violent, sudden revolution. It frequently seems that revolution is the fastest, easiest way, and might be the only way. However, experience everywhere shows that any revolution that has succeeded derives its legitimacy from itself and aims to perpetuate its power. How easy it is to justify this by saying that democracy has no meaning unless the 'old centres of

[1] The truest indication of the transformation of any phenomenon into a historical influence is the declaration by the enemies of this phenomenon of their deep belief in it!

power are eliminated', which requires the continuation of the revolution. There is only one Arab officer in modern Arab history who has fulfilled his promise to surrender power to an elected government after seizing control of the government by force. He is the Sudanese General ʿAbd al-Rahman Siwar al-Dhahab. This officer is the lone enlightened exception that proves the rule.

Hence, the government and the opposition in every Arab country must closely analyse the political situation and the available options. The government will discover that resisting pluralism is extremely difficult if not impossible. The opposition will discover that a democratic transformation cannot take place over several weeks or months. If what I have maintained is correct, the only way out would be through mutual concessions. The government would concede some of its authorities to elected bodies, and the opposition would abandon its quest to bring about the government's fall. Moreover, I further maintain that as long as these concessions are not made, according to the conditions and circumstances of each country, the Arab world will witness a series of violent changes. It is certain that these changes will produce new ruling classes. However, it is not certain that these classes will be more in favour of democracy than the old ruling classes.

If it is desired that the democratic transformation process succeed, in addition to mutual concessions it is necessary to start creating 'democratic awareness'. Democracy is not a formula but a process. It is not a document but a practice. It is not a law but a convention. No society can entrust all of its major affairs to an elected parliament and all of its minor affairs to appointed employees. 'Plurality' must be effected at all levels, the minor before the major. As long as the people of the village do not elect their village council, and the people of the district do not elect their district council, 'national' elections in the capital will be devoid of meaning. In Western democracy, where voting is the customary method of solving any problem, children are imbued with the tradition of voting from their earliest youth.[1] We in the Arab world cannot require an

---

[1] There is an American joke about a child who returns from school and tells his mother about an argument that had taken place about whether the frog which the biology teacher had brought to class was male or female. When his mother asked how it was settled, he answered simply: 'We voted of course!'

adult in his sixties to begin practising democracy. The process must begin in the elementary school, with elections to the school activities committees. The process must advance as the student advances. I personally believe that starting to train people in democracy is much more important than 'declaring' democracy. Every election that replaces an appointment – whether for the mayor of a village, the chairmanship of a board of directors of a co-operative, or the chairmanship of a merchants' guild – is a step in the right direction toward creating a healthy climate in which democracy can breathe.

If dialogue is the only alternative to an internal explosion in every Arab country, it is also the only alternative to tension in relations between Arab countries. In these circumstances, the only slogan more dangerous than 'May God forgive the past' is 'May God never forgive the past'. The first slogan means that we have not derived a single lesson from the crisis, and the second means that the Arab nation will remain an eternal prisoner of the crisis. We now need to understand how what happened did happen and how we can avoid repeating it. The only way to such knowledge is dialogue.

The dialogue must be based on a firm foundation, namely acceptance of the 'state' as the basic reality in the contemporary Arab world. It is useless to 'prove' that this or that country was created by colonialism, or that the borders of this or that state are artificial, or that the structure of this or that state is unsound. International society is based on the mutual recognition of sovereign states, regardless of how small or artificial they are. Arab political society must, for its part, recognize this fact conclusively and definitively. The Arab 'state' has proved its ability to remain steadfast in the face of any national plot that aims to eliminate it in the name of Arab unity. It has also proved its ability to confront any 'fundamentalist' plot that aims to liquidate it in the name of Islamic unity.

The acceptance of a state as an existing fact gives rise to another basic principle, which is 'non-intervention in internal affairs'. There is no doubt that the enticements to intervene are difficult to resist at times. Every revolution throughout history has resorted to the export of revolution to protect itself against real or unreal dangers. The export of revolution necessarily means intervention in the affairs of others. Every revolution throughout history has discovered that the export of

148

revolution, in the long term, is an adventure doomed to failure. A living example is provided by what we now see in Iran, where the revolution has turned into a state that is willing to talk with other countries after bitter, bloody experiences.

The Arab–Arab dialogue should begin on the basis of each state reassuring its 'neighbours' and 'sisters' about itself. This dialogue must be courageous, frank and comprehensive. The goal is not to return to old ways, but to develop new ways that are better than those which created, or contributed to the crisis.

Among the issues that should be treated in a frank dialogue is the 'distribution of Arab wealth'. This slogan, which assumes the form of 'Arab oil for the Arabs', has proved its ability to attract a great deal of support. However, the problem of 'the distribution of wealth' is thorny and cannot be solved by provocative slogans. Throughout human history, the distribution of wealth has been a moral, political, economic and social problem which no religion, philosophy or ideology has been able to ignore. Schools of thought on this matter include: the 'individualist' school, which permits the individual to hoard wealth to the extent of his ability without any responsibility being imposed on him in return; the 'collectivist' school (socialism), which limits the right of ownership to the community and denies it to the individual; and the 'compromise' school, which has attempted to balance the individual's right to personal property with the right of the community. The Islamic solution tries to achieve such a balance.

Islam has faced the income disparity problem courageously, aiming for a comprehensive solution but achieving, through laxity in application, only partial success. It has done so based on a two-part strategy: inheritance legislation and alms tax legislation. Inheritance legislation put an end to the pre-Islamic inheritance system, which denied women and young children any right to an inheritance and replaced it with a precise inheritance system that ensured the division of the largest estates after one or two generations (leading some orientalists to believe that Islam is inherently hostile to capitalism). The noble Quran details the provisions pertaining to inheritances, in contrast to other legislation in the Quran, which is recorded in outline but not detailed. (The other exception involving detailed legislation in the Quran relates to the rights and duties of women.)

The second part of the strategy is the alms tax. A major mistaken belief surrounds the alms tax, inasmuch as some (those who do not pay it!) consider it a paltry rate of tax. The source of this mistaken perception is the belief that this rate is levied on income, whereas in fact, it is levied on total wealth, according to the terms of Islamic law. Let us take the example of a person who owns property which is subject to the alms tax and which is valued at 1 million riyals. This person must pay an annual alms tax of 25,000 riyals. If this person was receiving an annual income of between 70,000 and 80,000 riyals, he would pay close to a third of his income in the alms tax annually, a rate that is consistent with the most modern and equitable tax systems.

Beyond this is the question of whether there are rights on wealth other than alms tax. Throughout our entire Islamic history, this has been, and it still is, an urgent and, vital question. The famous dispute between the venerable companions of the Prophet, 'Uthman Ibn 'Affan and Abu Dharr al-Ghaffari (a dispute which some wish to delete from our history, and which others wish to depict as a dispute between capitalism and socialism), is actually nothing but a legitimate difference in judgment between those who would limit rights on wealth to the alms tax, who included the third orthodox caliph ('Uthman), and those who would extend these rights beyond the alms tax, who included Abu Dharr.

If the issue of the distribution of wealth within the state is a thorny complicated issue, there is no doubt that the distribution of wealth across borders is even more complicated. Because the issue continues to be raised, it should be discussed on the basis of calm analysis, not misleading political slogans. This analysis must treat two basic elements. The first is the amount of aid which the oil-producing states can provide without damaging their economies and their citizens' well-being. (The United Nations has in the past recommended that each of the industrialized countries provide 1 per cent of their national income to aid the developing countries, but none of the industrialized countries attained this percentage). The second element is the best means for providing this aid.

Perhaps the ordinary Arab citizen would be amazed to know

that existing Arab development funds contain enormous sums that are seeking well studied projects to finance, but are not finding them. This writer was a member of the first board of directors of the Arab Investment Company, which is composed of a number of Arab states and was founded in the 1970s to finance development projects in the Arab world. The company began operating with a substantial amount of capital available to it. However, well-studied projects were rare. Sometimes the company was asked to participate to the amount of tens of millions of dollars in projects that had not been studied at all, and sometimes the 'study' consisted of limited information recorded on a single page.

Frequently, projects begin in the Arab world, and in the Third World in general, in the following way: the government decides to establish a project, say a cement factory. It contacts the companies possessing the relevant know-how and obtains technical specifications and estimated costs. It selects a site near the raw material and obtains the necessary financing. Before work begins, an official 'discovers' that the site lacks electricity, and the plan and costs are re-examined. Work begins and another official suggests that a temporary housing project be started for the workers, and this project is added. During the construction of the project, another official recommends permanent housing for the factory workers in the future, and the necessary amendments are incorporated. Then, someone else discovers that there are no roads leading to the factory and recommends building them. Another official uncovers a difficulty pertaining to the transport of the raw materials in vehicles and recommends the construction of a railway line for this purpose. Thus, the cost and implementation period are doubled. I have frequently entertained hopes of seeing a large Arab think-tank specialized in performing detailed feasibility studies on different projects throughout the Arab countries. The effect of such an organization on Arab development efforts can only be imagined by one who is familiar with the current shameful situation.

One of the problems frequently faced by aid donor states is the insistence of the recipient states on receiving aid in cash (to provide for the greatest measure of flexibility in dispensing it). However, such cash aid is not the best way from a development standpoint. Perhaps the time has come to establish an

Arab bank for development on the model of the World Bank, which would operate based on the same foundations and criteria. The elimination of 'flowery language' and the regulation of Arab aid on sound economic foundations would ensure the removal of difficulties for contributors and beneficiaries alike. It is to be hoped that current efforts to study the establishment of a Gulf fund will end up with an Arab bank for development.

Another issue related to this subject is the investment of oil proceeds in the West. Frequently, voices are raised in the Arab and Islamic worlds demanding that priority be given to the investment of these proceeds in Arab and Islamic economies, which need such investment more than the developed, Western economies. In principle, there is no objection to this change of direction. The real problem concerns guaranteeing a reasonable return on the investment (and the recovery of the invested capital itself). This is not an easy process given the difficult economic circumstances being experienced by the developing countries. The Arab economist who calls for the investment of Arab funds in the Arab countries is the first to hasten to place his personal investments in a safe place in the West. The cowardice of capital will not be remedied by friendly advice, but by effective guarantees.

The dialogue must also deal with joint Arab activity, for which the main instrument is the Arab League. In the 1950s, the political activity of the Arab League was limited to the conclusion of a number of treaties and alliances (which were ineffective). In the 1960s, the League's political role was limited to arranging truces between warring Arab camps when necessary. In the 1970s, the League's political role was limited to approving aid from the oil countries to the confrontation states. In the 1980s, the League proved to be completely ineffective. It should be acknowledged that all the Arab League's organizations have failed to formulate a united Arab strategy in the political and economic fields, and even in areas that are less sensitive, such as information, culture and tourism.

There has been an enormous gap between the world of theory (where the hypothetical supreme Arab interest prevails) and the world of reality (where the interest of each state prevails). The theoretical world has given rise to an enormous concentration of schemes for 'common Arab markets', 'joint, collective security pacts', and different types of 'Arab economic unity'. As for reality, it has not only proceeded in isolation from the world of theory, it has moved in the opposite direction, sometimes at high speed. Thus, we have seen that whenever a new resolution is issued to eliminate customs barriers, customs officials place greater restrictions on the exempted goods! Whenever a new communiqué is issued declaring a new Arab unity programme, an Arab state, or a group of states, severs relations with another state or group of Arab states. Whenever a statement is issued in support of the Palestinian cause, the sufferings of the 'supported' Palestinians in the Arab countries increase. Whenever a joint Arab project is established, existing Arab projects are disbanded.

The Arab League is called upon, in its new era, to declare the end of these contradictions. The only sound premise is realism, whereby each Arab country pursues its interests, not the nice dream of Arab unity. It is possible to form from the combination of individual Arab interests a broader Arab interest, not vice versa. The model of the European common market has proven that a state can preserve its personality, distinction, organizations, and the lion's share of its sovereignty while simultaneously participating in effective unified activity. This European model is worthy of the attention of Arab thinkers in the coming years.

The comprehensive dialogue must also treat the nature of the relation between Islam and Arabism. The experience of each Arab country has proven that it is impossible to divest the Arab masses of their Islamic beliefs in the name of nationalism. But it is doubtful whether these masses would follow the anti-Arab trend that employed Islamic slogans to strike at Arabism. Attempts to drive a wedge between Islam and Arabism began long ago and have not ceased. Their objective has been to sow discord between the two. These attempts, very unfortunately, strike a responsive chord in the heart of both the Islamic camp and the Arab camp, which is dangerous. The truth of the matter is that there is no contradiction between Islam and Arabism. No rational Arab would maintain that Arabism is an alternative to Islam as a religion. Nor would any rational Muslim assert that Islam is an eternal enemy of Arabism.

In the Quran, the word 'Arab' appears more than ten times (which compelled Colonel Mu'ammar al-Qadhdhafi to adopt his famous, erroneous theory, which is that the Quran was revealed exclusively to the Arabs). Islam, while clearly stipulating that the Arab has no superiority over the non-Arab, stipulates with the same clarity that both exist in the real world (Surah 'Fussilat' verse 41). Acknowledgement of the existence of 'Arabs' and 'non-Arabs' does not mean that Arabs are superior to non-Arabs. Rather, it means acknowledging a fact of human civilization and God's will for the world.

Islam treats 'Arabism' as a social phenomenon on a par with 'tribalism', 'the family', or 'customary law'. A number of precepts have developed from these phenomena, without anyone having said that 'tribalism', 'the family', or 'customary law' conflict with Islam. It suffices here to refer to the famous saying of the Prophet, which states that 'the leaders [of Islam] shall be from Quraysh [the Prophet's tribe].' The pioneering sociologist and outstanding legist, Ibn Khaldun, believed that this saying of the Prophet was more of an expression of the political reality during the days of the Prophet than the declaration of a permanent legal principle (and a number of contemporary Muslim legists understand this saying of the Prophet in the same way). However, does it not seem strange that some regard Arabism as conflicting with Islam while believing that the next leader of the entire Islamic nation must be of the tribe of Quraysh?!

There must be a broad dialogue between Arab intellectuals. The Gulf crisis proved anew that the ability of Arab intellectuals to differ is no less than that of governments. It showed that the ideal 'intellectual', who is free of considerations of time and place, exists only in the imagination (of intellectuals themselves). The crisis has proved that the intellectual is a normal individual with an unusual education. In other words, he carries within him all the shortcomings and human weaknesses of the ordinary person.

Throughout the crisis, there was a feverish search for the ideal intellectual who would adopt an exemplary position despite all the political pressures. The search ended in bitter disappointment. Those who sided with Iraq were amazed to find a single Arab intellectual whose position differed from their position. Those who opposed Iraq's occupation of Kuwait were shocked to discover that a large number of Arab intellectuals were lining up behind the occupier of Kuwait. There was nothing to justify the feverish search and great disappointment of hopes. The Arab intellectual did not adopt a utopian position, but one that was dictated by his political, social, economic, party or tribal affiliation. The desired discussion among Arab intellectuals must be based on this realistic foundation, not on imaginary roles for imaginary intellectuals.

The anticipated Arab dialogue must include the relation of the Arabs to the wider world, particularly Western culture. There is no doubt that a painful historical legacy determines relations between Islam and the West. The peak bitterness of the legacy was reached in the wars of the Crusades, which many view as never having ended. Many who applauded Saddam Hussein were attracted by the courage of a small Arab country standing alone against the flood of Western civilization. This emotional attitude is understandable. However, emotions cannot be adopted as a basis for dealing with civilizations. The 'fundamentalist' preacher on the mosque pulpit can declare an immediate armed holy war against non-Muslims (as many preachers did during the crisis), excite the emotions of listeners, and enjoy great popularity among them. The Arab nationalist can strike a resonant chord when he declares that the Arabs are subject to a conspiracy to liquidate them by the other peoples of the world. However, slogans which seem rousing and eloquent in a sermon or a communiqué are transformed into certain suicide if they become the basis of the Arabs' behaviour in contemporary international society.

A reasonable person should not take all that was said before or during the crisis seriously. Many acts and utterances were a product of the crisis; they have disappeared or will disappear with the end of the crisis. However, the reasonable mind must not ignore all the effects of the crisis. It has been shown, without a doubt, that hidden and suppressed within the hearts of the Arabs are feelings whose presence was not imagined by anyone before. Dealing with these feelings is much more important than restoring normal diplomatic relations between governments. Hence, this call for a dialogue is a call to use the crisis to the advantage of the Arab future, instead of permitting it to destroy this future. I maintain that, until this courageous, honest dialogue begins, the calm that prevails in the Arab world at present will be a mere truce that will sooner

or later end with a destructive storm that will be more serious
than the one which blew over the Arab world on that hot day
in the summer of 1990.